PAST and PRESENT

No 63

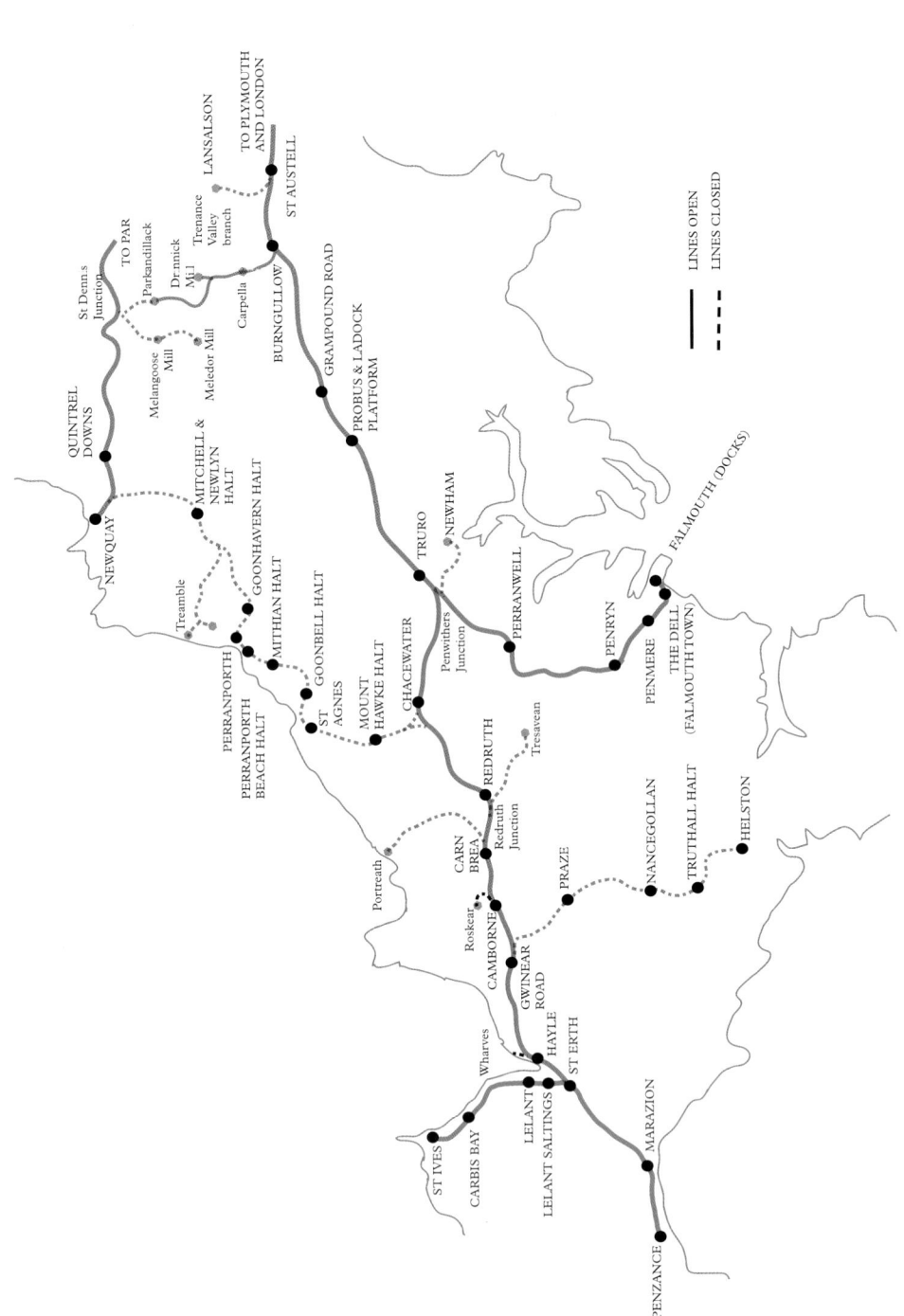

Map of the area covered by this book, showing locations featured or referred to in the text.

PAST and PRESENT

No 63
West Cornwall

David Mitchell

Past & Present Publishing Ltd

© David Mitchell 2010

All rights reserved. No part of this publication may be reproduced, stored in a retrieval system or transmitted, in any form or by any means, electronic, mechanical, photocopying, recording or otherwise, without prior permission in writing from Past & Present Publishing Ltd.

First published in 2010

British Library Cataloguing in Publication Data

A catalogue record for this book is available from the British Library.

ISBN 978 1 85895 267 3

Past & Present Publishing Ltd
The Trundle
Ringstead Road
Great Addington
Kettering
Northants NN14 4BW

Tel/Fax: 01536 330588
email: sales@nostalgiacollection.com
Website: www.nostalgiacollection.com

Printed and bound in the Czech Republic

ST AUSTELL: Long-standing Truro-based No 1023 *County of Oxford* **approaches the station with an up train on a summer Saturday in 1958. It has just passed Trenance Junction, a quarter of a mile away, the southern end of the short Trenance Valley branch. A signal box had once been located at the junction, but this was replaced by a ground frame in 1949 when the former access to the branch from both up and down lines was singled. Henceforth trains both to and from this mineral branch had to run over the up main from St Austell. Just beyond this junction is the 206-yard-long St Austell Viaduct, about half a mile from the base of which was the terminus of the 3½-mile-long Pentewan Railway. Opened in 1829 as a 4-foot-gauge horse-drawn operation, it was converted to 2ft 6in gauge in 1874 and worked by steam locos. With the main aim of transporting china clay from pits north of St Austell (particularly in the Trenance Valley) to Pentewan's harbour, it suffered by not directly serving the clay dries, and also from recurrent silting of the harbour, and closed in 1918.**
  On 18 September 2008 'Sprinter' No 150246 approaches forming the 1142 Penzance to Newton Abbot service. *P. Q. Treloar/DHM*

CONTENTS

Introduction	7
St Austell to Truro	9
Trenance Valley branch	34
Burngullow to St Dennis Junction	38
Retew branch	50
Routes to Newquay	54
Truro to Falmouth	70
Chacewater to Penzance	80
Helston branch	109
Hayle wharves branch	115
St Ives branch	119
Index of locations	128

BEACON AND HIGH STREET SIDINGS: The china clay industry played an important role in the development of the railway network in the eastern part of the area covered in this book. On 13 July 1961 0-6-0PTs Nos 9755 and 1624 are descending from Drinnick Mill to Burngullow with more than 20 loaded wagons and will shortly pass under the A3058 road. The train has not long shunted three empty wagons into New Carpella siding and is now continuing at no more than 10mph due to a ruling gradient between here and Burngullow of up to 1 in 46. Beacon Siding is in the right foreground, but appears to be disused and was removed in June 1963. Curving away to the right is High Street Siding, also serving a clay loading wharf; both this siding and its headshunt are on the pre-'Carpella Gap' alignment (see also page 39). *Peter W. Gray*

GWINEAR ROAD: Horticultural produce was for a long time a lucrative traffic in west Cornwall. On 9 April 1960 2-6-2T No 4564 is in Gwinear Road sidings with cattle wagons that will be loaded with boxes of broccoli. To the left, the rear of a broccoli special from Ponsandane yard can be glimpsed on the up main behind 4-6-0 No 4083 *Abbotsbury Castle*. *P. Q. Treloar*

Introduction

Mention Cornwall to many people today and they probably think of its extensive and varied coastline, wild moorland landscapes and mild climate. Although they may be aware of a mining history, it might surprise them to learn that the county's economy was one of the first in the world to industrialise, with the early application of steam power enabling the development of deep mining and placing the Duchy in the forefront of technological innovation. The winning of tin and copper goes back at least to the Bronze Age, but by the early decades of the 19th century there were more than 200 mines employing 30,000 men, women and children in the production of two-thirds of the world supply of copper.

James Watt's engines had arrived in the county in the 1770s, but Cornish engineers used the experience that they had gained from working in the busiest and richest mining field in the world to develop steam power further, and once Watt's patents had expired they competed to perfect the Cornish beam engine. The most renowned of these engineers was Richard Trevithick, born near Carn Brea in 1771, who built a high-pressure engine that was not only more powerful than the old low-pressure engines, but also smaller and cheaper. This development enabled shafts to be sunk deeper into the ground, and even under the sea bed. Trevithick was also responsible for the invention of a steam road carriage that was trialled in Camborne in 1801, and his Penydarren engine of 1804 was the first successful railway locomotive.

The enormous demand for engines and other mining machinery, both locally and for export across the globe, led to the establishment of at least 30 brass and iron foundries near the mining centres. Trevithick's father-in-law, John Harvey, transformed his blacksmith's shop into one of the biggest engineering firms in the country and played an important role in the growth of Hayle as an industrial port. Renowned for its mine pumps, the company's last great undertaking was the provision of beam engines for the Severn Tunnel's Sudbrook pumping station; these kept the tunnel clear of water from 1886 until 1961.

Early railway development in west Cornwall was concerned with conveying copper and tin ore from the mining heartland to the ports, with coal imports for the mine engines an important balancing traffic. The earliest of these was the horse-drawn Poldice Tramway, which ran from a mining area east of Redruth to the small north coast harbour of Portreath, and was in partial use by 1809. This was eventually joined by the Redruth & Chasewater Railway, which opened in 1826, with steam locomotives introduced in 1854. The Hayle Railway was of more significance in the long term as much of it was to form the basis of the West Cornwall Railway, itself eventually becoming part of today's main line through the county.

With Cornwall's minerals being sent away by sea, there was little demand from the mine-owners for improved transport eastwards, and the initial proposals for such a railway emanated from interests in Falmouth who were concerned that the town's status as a mail packet station was threatened through the building of railways to other ports nearer London. However, by the time Falmouth did eventually get its railway, the packets had long since transferred to Southampton.

Copper-mining reached its peak in 1856, particularly in the Chacewater and Camborne area, and there was then a steady decline, mainly due to cheaper and more accessible sources abroad. As the industry collapsed there was a mass emigration of miners and their families to these newly discovered mining areas in the Americas, South Africa and Australia. The disaster was alleviated in part by the development of tin lodes found beneath the copper ones, but this activity reached its peak in the 1870s with a steady decline thereafter; though Cornwall's last tin mine did not close until 1998.

The opening of the Cornwall Railway in 1859 provided a connection with the rest of England, and gave hope both as a reliable employer itself and as a creator of fresh business opportunities. Although the copper and tin mines had had little need for the new railway, some of the miners found work in the expanding china clay industry, an activity that did benefit from the developing railway network. Improved transport and the warm equable climate made it possible for the farmers of west Cornwall to turn their fields into market gardens supplying potatoes, broccoli and other vegetables to London and elsewhere. A similar market for flowers followed, though these were mainly grown on the Isles of Scilly where the harvest began during the winter months. The coming of the railway also helped the fishing industry, and in 1860 fish to the value of £80,000 was sent to London. The other main development, and possibly the most important in the long term, was in the holiday trade and the opening up of the county to popular, organised tourism.

Apart from the loss of certain mineral lines and a few little-used stations, west Cornwall's railway network remained intact until 1962-63, when both the Helston branch and Chacewater to Newquay line were closed. Both these losses just pre-dated Dr Beeching's plan, but his report did propose the closure of the St Ives branch and all the intermediate stations on the Par to Newquay route; however, all were subsequently reprieved. Five stations on the main line were not so fortunate, but Hayle was also reprieved and is one of seven such stations within this title's area that are still open today. Three passenger branch lines are also still operating; for the first time since I began compiling volumes in this series I was able to travel by rail when obtaining about a half of the 'present' photos for this book. My journeys over these fascinating and picturesque routes were undertaken on what appeared to be a well-used and largely efficient railway.

In closing, I should like to thank all of the 'past' photographers who are credited individually within, Geoff Lendon and Richard Woodley for providing photographs, Nigel Tregoning for scanning some of the images and taking two updated 'present' pictures, and Peter Gray for both information and his comments on the manuscript.

BIBLIOGRAPHY

Becket, W. S. *Operation Cornwall* (Xpress, 2007)
Bennett, Alan *The GWR in Mid Cornwall* (Kingfisher, 1988)
    The GWR in West Cornwall (Kingfisher, 1988)
Cooke, R. A. *Track Layout Diagrams of the GWR, Section 10* (R. A. Cooke, 1977)
    Atlas of the GWR (Wild Swan, 1988)
Dart, Maurice *West Cornwall Mineral Railways* (Middleton, 2005)
    Cornwall Narrow Gauge (Middleton, 2005)
Gray, Peter W. *Rail Trails: South West* (Silver Link, 1992)
    Steam in Cornwall (Ian Allan, 1993)
    Steam Around Devon & Cornwall (Ian Allan, 2001)
Jenkins, S. C. and Langley, R. C. *The West Cornwall Railway* (Oakwood, 2002)
Mitchell, David *British Railways Past & Present No 17: Cornwall* (Past & Present, 1993)
    British Railways Past & Present No 54: East Cornwall (Past & Present, 2006)
Mitchell, Vic and Smith, Keith *St Austell to Penzance* (Middleton, 2001)
    Branch Lines to Newquay (Middleton, 2001)
    Branch Lines to Falmouth, Helston & St Ives (Middleton, 2001)
Reade, Lewis *Branch Line Memories, Vol 1 Great Western* (Atlantic, 1983)
    The Branch Lines of Cornwall (Atlantic, 1984)
Vaughan, John *Branches & Byways: Cornwall* (OPC, 2002)
    Rails to Newquay (Oakwood, 2008)
    An Illustrated History of the Cornish Main Line (OPC, 2009)
Walnutt-Read, A. *BR Steam Operating: Plymouth-Penzance* (Xpress)

GWR Service Timetable Appendices 1945 (Bradford Barton reprint)
Plymouth Traffic District Sectional Appendix (BR June 1960).

St Austell to Truro

ST AUSTELL: The broad gauge Cornwall Railway obtained its Act of Parliament in 1846, but financial difficulties meant that it was not actually opened for passengers until 4 May 1859, when services started from the South Devon Railway's terminus at Plymouth Millbay to Truro. Although originally promoted by local men, it was partly financed by the Great Western, Bristol & Exeter and South Devon railways and was leased to and operated by these companies at the time of its opening. The eastern approach to one of the original stations is made through a deep cutting and D1010 *Western Campaigner* is seen on 10 September 1971 with 1V76, the 1025 Manchester Piccadilly to Penzance service. The track on the left is a bi-directional goods loop, about a quarter of a mile long, which runs from the station to the town's third goods depot. Known in official documents as the New Yard, it provided greatly enhanced facilities when opened on 2 November 1931.

The loop has been disconnected from the main line at its eastern end, but still exists as an emergency siding. No 150233 forms the 1244 Plymouth to Penzance service on 18 September 2008. *Both DHM*

ST AUSTELL: Looking the other way from the same road bridge on 21 March 1972, Laira's Sulzer Type 2 No 7506 is marshalling empty coal wagons in sidings located on the up side of the station. The future No 25156 has drawn the wagons from New Yard over the loop line and, after attaching the SR bogie brake-van, will head eastwards up the main line. A cattle dock was once located just to the left of the third wagon, while the siding to the left of this was then still used to load cars on to Motorail trains.

General goods traffic in New Yard ended in May 1968, but domestic coal traffic continued until 1985. The site of that yard has since been redeveloped, and is now in both commercial and residential use. The last Motorail service to London ran in 1984, and only stubs of the former sidings remain today, operated from a ground frame, which also gives access to the emergency siding. No 150249 leaves forming the 1255 Penzance to Plymouth service on 18 September 2008. *John Medley/DHM*

ST AUSTELL: The Bristol & Exeter and South Devon railways amalgamated with the Great Western in 1876 and 1878 respectively, the latter becoming the sole lessee of the Cornwall Railway, which itself was amalgamated on 1 July 1889. Conversion to standard gauge followed on 20-21 May 1892 and the line from Par to here was doubled in October 1893. 0-6-0PT No 9755 pauses in the up platform with a loaded clay train from Drinnick Mill in June 1958; on arrival back at St Blazey, the loco will have completed an almost day-long circuit, having operated via St Dennis Junction on its outward journey.

In a second 'past' picture, D1029 *Western Legionnaire* arrives with 1B16, the 1755 Penzance to Bristol Temple Meads service, on 10 September 1971. The main station building is on the down side, while further to the left the roof of the large second goods shed can be noted. This opened in about 1899 but closed in 1931 when the more spacious seven-siding New Yard was opened. The building was subsequently used as a bus garage, but was demolished later in the 1970s. *David Lawrence/DHM*

ST AUSTELL: The town grew to become the commercial and administrative centre of the china clay industry, and is now the largest in Cornwall; its population at the 2001 census was 22,658, with a current estimate of 28,000. The station is located on high ground north of the town centre, with a bus station conveniently located outside the main entrance. A Western National service to Foxhole, Nanpean and St Dennis awaits departure on 12 May 1951. These villages are in the heart of china clay country and although all have been close to a railway for about 150 years, they have never had the benefit of a passenger service. No 1611 is almost new, and has a Bristol LWL5G chassis with an Eastern Coachworks body.

The station footbridge links these views, but the main Victorian station building was demolished in 1999 and a new, more spacious structure opened on 8 June 2000. Work was being undertaken on modernising the bus station in September 2008 – what is now called a 'public transport interchange'. *J. H. Bamsey/DHM*

ST AUSTELL: Laira's 'Modified Hall' No 7909 *Heveningham Hall* drifts into the up platform in the summer of 1958, not long before its transfer to Westbury shed. The 43-lever signal box is largely hidden by the second coach; it was erected in 1899 when the line to Burngullow was doubled and is positioned near the site of the first goods shed. It replaced an earlier box located at the west end of the down platform. Beyond it is a footbridge that was previously at St Blazey station, but was moved here to replace a level crossing in 1931.

The signal box closed in March 1980 when its semaphores were replaced by colour light signals, controlled initially from Burngullow box. However, the structure is still standing and is being passed by power car No 43165 heading the 1600 Penzance to Paddington HST on 18 September 2008. The former siding area to the right is now used for car parking. *Norman Simmons/DHM*

ST AUSTELL: 4-6-0 No 6869 *Resolven Grange* waits for the road with a stopping service bound for its Penzance home on 12 May 1951, while on the right Laira-based large 'Prairie' tank No 5148 has recessed its down freight on the longer of two sidings located next to the second goods shed. The far end of this siding was 'filled in' between the rails to enable road traffic in the station forecourt, particularly buses, to pass over it. A wheelstop with padlock and key was available for each of the rails, and fitted when the end of the siding was not required for rail traffic.

This siding was removed in 1965, with the other one subsequently realigned to allow for an extended walkway to the barrow crossing, this being needed when the up platform was extended in 1971. On 20 February 1973 D1012 *Western Firebrand* leaves with 1V76, the 0915 Liverpool to Penzance train. *J. H. Bamsey/DHM*

ST AUSTELL: Viewed from the footbridge seen on page 13, an unusual visitor from Old Oak Common shed, 4-6-0 No 5987 *Brocket Hall*, is departing on what is thought to be a summer Saturday in 1958, quite possibly 2 August, when this engine was observed working in the county. Since leaving Par at almost sea level, the train has climbed for 4¼ miles at a ruling gradient of 1 in 55 with varying lengths of lesser gradients, and now faces a further climb of up to 1 in 84 for 1¾ miles to the summit at Burngullow. The vans to the left of the engine are on a short siding that ran up to the signal box.

The extended up platform now covers the site of this short siding, and the remaining down-side siding was removed in 1979. The 0730 Paddington to Penzance HST (power cars 43169 and 43024) leaves on 18 September 2008. *P. Q. Treloar/DHM*

BURNGULLOW: The Cornwall Railway opened a single-platform station here on 1 February 1863, but after the line was doubled it was not possible to build a second platform due to the presence of four pan-kilns, which were built at about the same time to serve the massive Blackpool china clay pit, just to the north of here. The station was therefore re-sited 11 chains to the west. On 28 September 1978 No 37267 has just arrived from Drinnick Mill with loaded 'clayhoods', while No 25206 is running 'light engine' over the down main. The 'Rat' had earlier worked the sidings north of Drinnick, then piloted the Class 37 from there. A clay loading platform can be noted above No 25206, with the original station house in view on the right. The massive concrete silos were constructed in the 1960s to handle spray-dried clay, but were to prove to be 'white elephants'.

    The line from here to Probus was singled in October 1986 as an economy measure, with the down rails removed. Some of the track is still in situ, however, on 16 September 1987 as No 50020 *Revenge* speeds past with the 0645 Swindon to Penzance service.

The sidings were completely remodelled early in 1989 to serve a new china clay slurry plant, the location then being called Blackpool. The kilns had closed by then, but their linhays were used for the storage of clay dried elsewhere. In the third view, the building on the left is the slurry loading shed, while the other modern building contains plant for cleaning the interiors of slurry tank wagons. The new Class 66 took over the operation of clay trains in 1999, but there was a delay in their working the Parkandillack branch due to restrictions over a bridge just to the north of Drinnick Mill. On 9 September 1999 No 37688 has arrived from Parkandillack with loaded CDA wagons, but will swap with No 66128, which is arriving with a rake of empties from Carne Point.

The 'sheds' were soon cleared to cross the bridge, but at a maximum speed of 10mph. However, the slurry traffic did not develop as expected and production here ceased in September 2003. Although the sidings still see some use, including the loading of sand trains and repair of wagons, all china clay activity has now ceased and plans have been published to redevelop the whole site, with a new station provided. On 30 May 2006 steam returned to the Parkandillack branch for the first time in more than 44 years; Standard 2-6-0 No 76079 is tailing the returning 'China Clay Pony'. *All DHM*

BURNGULLOW: The second station opened on 1 August 1901, with an up platform considerably shorter than the down due to the pre-existing Newquay & Cornwall Junction Railway route to Drinnick Mill, which had opened in 1869. A branch platform was unnecessary as the latter has never had a passenger service. The station is pictured here in possibly about 1920. The engine shed opened with the N&CJR but was closed by at least 1906 and was demolished in 1929. To the right of this are Burngullow West clay dries, served by a siding off the branch from 1898 until 1974.

With no significant population in the area it is perhaps not surprising that the station was closed on 14 September 1931. No 66078 eases off the branch on 18 November 2008 with four covered hoppers from Central Treviscoe. After a break it will work forward as 6C41, the Burngullow to Exeter Riverside service. A heavily overgrown up-side station building survives, and can be noted to the left of the wagons. *Author's collection/DHM*

BURNGULLOW: On 4 May 1991 No 50008 *Thunderer* heads for Penzance with 1Z16, the 'Cornish Centurion II' from Manchester Piccadilly, tailed by No 50015 *Valiant*; the railtour had earlier visited Carne Point and the Parkandillack branch. The road overbridge visible in the background is where the photos seen on pages 16-18 were taken. Also just discernible on the right is the signal box. This opened with the second station in 1901, being located at the west end of the down platform. It had 31 levers and was originally known as Burngullow West, due to the existence of an East box in the years from 1899 to 1935. It closed on 5 October 1986 when the main line was singled, signalling in the area then coming under the control of Par box. Clearly visible to the left of *Thunderer* is the formation of the up refuge siding.

The closed box was used by permanent way staff until destroyed by arsonists. The National Railway Museum's No 3440 *City of Truro* provides a splendid spectacle as it speeds westward with 1Z40, the 1040 Plymouth to Truro special on 30 November 2004, organised by Network Rail to mark the official reopening of the double-track section to Probus and carrying industry representatives and guests. It will shortly pass a Virgin Trains 'Voyager', the first such to pass on the reinstated section. *Both DHM*

BURNGULLOW: Turning the other way, No 47090 is heading east on 11 April 1984 with empty fuel tanks from Long Rock and cement empties from Chacewater. The rake of 'clayhoods' is on the up refuge siding. The train has just been brought off the Parkandillack branch by No 37176 and shunted into this siding. In steam days the refuge was deemed long enough to hold an engine, brake-van and 41 wagons.

With the main line singled, and the refuge lifted in about 1989, the view is somewhat different on 4 May 1991 as No 47813 powers the 0913 Penzance to Edinburgh 'Cornishman'.

Loco-hauled cross-country workings ended in 2002, and today's equivalent, a 'Voyager' set, forms the 0930 Penzance to Manchester Piccadilly service on 18 November 2008. Work started on the £14.3 million project to re-double almost 7 miles of line in early 2004, and was completed on time and on budget. Double-track from 1898, the line had been singled as part of industry cutbacks to save money. Although such a large investment in Cornwall's railway is to be welcomed, it has to be recognised that it was only justified as late running caused by this bottleneck had knock-on effects between Reading and Paddington, and as far as Birmingham. *All DHM*

On 3 January 1957, when a ganger was inspecting his 'length' just over a mile west of here at Dowgas, he found a gaping hole in the '6-foot' between the up and down tracks. It turned out to be a disused tin mine shaft of some depth, and all traffic was immediately stopped. The 'Cornish Riviera Limited' was about to leave Truro, but was sent back to Chacewater from where it travelled eastwards via Newquay. This was the only diversion, and all other trains were stopped at St Austell and Truro, with a bus service operating in between. Single-line working was resumed during the same afternoon, however, and both tracks were opened by the next day. The extent of the remedial work is not clear, but one suspects that a similar event today would lead to a closure measured in weeks rather than hours! One benefit of the 1986 singling was that only one train at a time would pass this sensitive location, but for many years the track was heavily braced as a precaution against subsidence. When the second track was reinstated, attention was paid to this problem and both trackbeds were reinforced with concrete raft capping. A mine shaft near the line was also capped.

GRAMPOUND ROAD: Opening with the Cornwall Railway, this station was sited largely in a cutting, about 4½ miles west of Burngullow. The village of Grampound can be found on the main road from St Austell to Truro, more than 2 miles to the south-east. A small community grew here, comprising two hotels and a number of dwellings. In this undated view from a road overbridge, the 27-lever signal box and main station building can be noted on the up platform, with the substantial goods shed beyond. Out of sight on the right is a two-siding goods yard on the down side. The station served an agricultural area and handled a fair amount of livestock and other agricultural traffic. Prior to the introduction of passenger services to Newquay, this was the railhead for the north coast resort, with a horse-drawn coach service running via St Columb.

Goods facilities were withdrawn on 1 June 1964, with all sidings at the east end of the station taken out of use three months later. Passenger services ceased from 5 October that year. An up refuge siding was provided at the west end, but this was taken out of use in 1966. The signal box closed on 2 June 1972. The up platform is still largely intact on 11 April 1984, as No 50014 *Warspite* passes with the 0750 Bristol Temple Meads to Penzance train.

In a scene from the 'modern' single-track era, Hunslet-Barclay Nos 20904 *Janis* and 20901 *Nancy* top and tail the Chipman's weedkilling train on 5 April 1991. The train was based at Horsham in West Sussex and at that time made an annual visit to Cornwall. The single-line section extended for a further 2 miles or so to Probus. Almost a mile further west, Probus & Ladock Platform had been open from 1908 to 1957.

Today housing has been erected on the site of the up goods yard. No 150339 passes forming the 1038 Plymouth to Penzance service on 18 November 2008. *Lens of Sutton Association/DHM/Ian Cavill/DHM*

TRURO: After a crew change, Hawksworth's 4-6-0 No 1001 *County of Bucks* awaits departure from Platform 4 with the 3.40pm Penzance to Paddington perishables on 9 September 1961. The 45-lever East signal box is in view. The coaches visible beyond the box are in a siding adjacent to the small down goods yard. Just in front of the engine is the east end of the 1,200-foot-long up loop, the track beyond this leading to the up and down goods loops. The parapet of the 268-yard-long Carvedras Viaduct can be glimpsed to the right of the cattle wagons; a short distance beyond this the 'County' will also cross the 437-yard Truro Viaduct, the longest on the former Cornwall Railway.

This platform was used by up main-line trains until May 1971 when it was relegated to a siding. East box has controlled all the area's signalling since November of that year, when the West and Penwithers Junction boxes were closed; a second-hand 51-lever frame was imported from Bristol East Depot to cater for the new arrangements. Unusually the signalman has his back to the trains when working the frame, as the original frame was still in situ when the new one was installed at the back of the box. A new level crossing was also provided to give access to the goods yard. The new signalling at Penryn is also controlled from this box.
Peter W. Gray/DHM

TRURO: The Cornwall Railway's station was located on high ground to the north-west of the town centre. The station evolved during the 19th century and today's facility basically dates from work completed in 1900, though the platforms were lengthened at the west end in 1913. Platform 2 was used by down main-line services, and No 4548 is heading the 5.18pm stopper to Penzance on 24 July 1957. This train connected with the 9.00am Wolverhampton to Penzance 'Cornishman', the latter calling only at St Erth on its journey westwards from here. The stock on the right is in Platform 1, the Falmouth branch bay. Our view is from Platform 3, which was used by Newquay and Falmouth branch services. Rather unusually the station has two covered footbridges, both in view.

Down main-line trains still use Platform 2, and No 150219 is leaving as the 1244 Plymouth to Penzance service on 23 September 2008. Platform 3 is now used by all up services, and can also again accommodate Falmouth trains from May 2009. *Peter W. Gray/DHM*

TRURO was given City status in 1877 and three years later work began on the construction of a cathedral. Cornwall County Council's headquarters are located here and Truro is the commercial and cultural capital of the Duchy with a population of 20,920 at the 2001 census. This was an important railway centre and traditionally the busiest station in Cornwall, with two branch services starting here, one to the south coast port of Falmouth and the other to the resort of Newquay on the Atlantic coast. Pannier tank No 4622 waits with a train for Falmouth on Whit Monday, 6 June 1960.

On hire to First Great Western, Arriva Trains No 150267 is about to depart as the 1429 service to Falmouth Docks on 23 September 2008. *Derek Frost/DHM*

TRURO: A timber-built two-road broad-gauge engine shed was located to the north of the station until its closure in 1900. The site was then developed into a sizeable goods yard, which ran parallel to the station. Looking east on 22 September 1970, No D6319 is in the eight-siding yard; the four tracks on the right are the up and down goods loops, the up loop and the up main, with Platform 4 just out of sight. The loco will spend the day out-stationed at Truro and work trips as required to the various goods depots that survived at that time, such as Newham, Penryn, Falmouth Docks and Chacewater.

Track rationalisation in the following year included removal of four of the sidings; the down goods loop, up loop and up main were also truncated at the new level crossing previously mentioned. The remaining access from the east end of the yard to the main line was removed in 1988. Today only two of the sidings remain in use, ostensibly for civil engineering purposes, and a car park covers much of the site. On 30 November 2004 No 37261 is backing on to the empty stock that formed *City of Truro*'s special working.
John Medley/DHM

TRURO: 0-6-0PT No 3709 makes a spirited departure from Platform 1 on 9 July 1960, while in the foreground 'Castle' Class No 5058 *Earl of Clancarty* is double-headed with No 6825 *Llanvair Grange* on the late-running down 'Cornishman'. The pannier tank and sister engine No 5744 are within days of their transfer from Didcot shed, and both have the spark-arresting chimneys that were fitted during the Second World War to allow them to shunt at Didcot's ordnance depot. However the spark arrestors were found to have such a bad effect on steaming that the apparatus was soon removed, leaving the locos with only their somewhat ugly chimney liners. Photographs of No 3709 in this later condition can be seen on Pages 97 and 101 of *British Railways Past & Present No 17*.

On 30 November 2004 *City of Truro* blows off steam as 'Sprinter' No 150265 arrives forming the 1308 Penzance to Exeter St David's service. The photos on pages 27 to 29 were all taken from a lengthy lattice bridge that carries a public footpath over the west end of the platforms and goods yard. *Peter W. Gray/DHM*

TRURO: Looking to the right of the previous view, we see 2-6-2T No 4574 entering the yard via the up goods loop on 21 September 1959 with a local trip working from Camborne and Redruth. The track in the left foreground is the up main, running through Platform 4. Note the changes made to the signalling in the short period between this photo and the 1960 one on the opposite page. The 'backing' signal seen here is replaced by the normal one seen the following year, presumably to allow departure westwards from No 4, and the 'cut-out' speed restriction signs have also arrived in the later view. The 49-lever West box can be noted in both photos, but here the stone-built engine shed is visible in the background. The three-road running shed, offices and stores are partly hidden by the box. Further to the right is the single-road repair shop with its higher roof, and adjoining this are three further roads that served as a carriage & wagon shop. To the right of these are six sidings used to provide additional stabling facilities for both passenger and goods stock.

The 'rationalised' scene from 2 August 2009 includes No 221122 approaching Platform 3 forming the 0930 Penzance to Glasgow service. The brand-new lower-quadrant semaphore signal immediately to the right of the 'Voyager' has been installed to enable Falmouth trains to depart from this platform. *P. Q. Treloar/Nigel Tregoning*

TRURO: The lattice footbridge forms a backdrop to this view of a trio of tank engines on 18 September 1957. Truro's 2-6-2T No 4508, on the left, has a shunters' truck and two brake-vans attached, with shed-mate 0-6-0PT No 8465 to its right. In the foreground Penzance-based No 8473 is in the down bay, presumably on a Falmouth train. For many years the mainstay of local station pilot and yard work had been elderly pannier tanks, the last in a long line being No 1782, which was built at Wolverhampton as a saddle tank in 1893, and finally withdrawn from here in November 1950. Replacements came in the form of new '94XX' Class engines, and up to six of this type were stationed here until the first diesel shunters arrived in 1958. To justify this glut of locos, they were often used to help out the more usual 'Prairie' tanks on the Falmouth branch.

Inevitable growth on the embankment precludes an exact facsimile today, but No 3440 *City of Truro* is seen from a little further west on 30 November 2004. *P. Q. Treloar/DHM*

TRURO: Shortly before being transferred to Laira, No 6805 *Broughton Grange* is on its home depot on 10 June 1958, at the head of what appears to be a rake of empty loco-coal wagons. Just beyond it is another 4-6-0, No 6931 *Aldborough Hall*, another engine that will soon be on the move, this time to St Blazey. The stone-built coal stage is on the right, complete with its 45,000-gallon water tank; the wagon road incline is clearly visible. On the left the main line climbs at a gradient of 1 in 60 towards Highertown Tunnel.

After closure of the shed, the site was redeveloped, with warehousing erected. However, a siding was retained and was used for inbound fertiliser loads. This traffic ended in 1993, but the decaying siding remains in situ. *P. K. Tunks/DHM*

TRURO SHED: Opening in 1900, Truro's second depot came under the Newton Abbot Division and was coded 83F in the British Railways era. During 1959 the three roads in the running shed were reduced to two, with an extension erected at the front of the shed to accommodate soon-to-arrive diesel multiple units. This rear view from 6 June 1960 includes the running shed and coal stage, with No 5515 the closest of a group of engines in the holding sidings. This 'Prairie' tank was based here throughout the 1950s, but was to be withdrawn from Laira shed in the following year. It is standing on track that leads to the 65-foot turntable, which had replaced a 55-foot model in 1924. The allocation at this time comprised 'Manor' 4-6-0s Nos 7812/13 and 20, 'Granges' Nos 6823/28, 2-6-2Ts Nos 4108, 4574/87/93, 5509/15/37/38/46/52 and 62, 0-6-0PTs Nos 3702, 4622, 6770 and 8486, and diesel shunters Nos D3509/10.

32

The shed closed to steam in March 1962 when its two remaining steam engines were transferred away (No 4673 to Taunton and No 5744 to Westbury), leaving the aforementioned diesel shunters as the only locos still allocated here. However, withdrawn pannier tank No 8408 arrived to act as a stationary boiler, and remained until May 1963. The depot was re-coded 84C in September 1963, but closed completely in October 1965. The same view today is hidden by trees, but in a telephoto lens picture from 20 February 1973 the roof of a warehouse under construction can be noted. A down train is signalled out of the station and No D1040 *Western Queen* will follow with a fuel tank for Long Rock, and a rake of loaded Presflo cement wagons bound for Chacewater.
Derek Frost/DHM

Trenance Valley branch

BOJEA SIDINGS: Construction work started in 1913 on the only china clay branch to be built by the Great Western Railway, but the advent of the Great War delayed progress and the first half-mile section from Trenance Junction to Bojea did not open until 1 May 1920. The sidings are seen from the north end on 11 May 1968. On the left is the running line, then No 1 siding, which had to be kept clear for running-round purposes; the wagon is on No 2 siding. There had been two further sidings to the right but these were removed in 1964. The massive Carlyon Farm kiln, the largest ever built, is in the distance. This was served by a further loop siding from its completion in February 1921 until closure in 1964.

The formation from near the site of Trenance Junction to the southern part of the sidings is now a cycleway, but the northern part is occupied by a fuel distribution depot and the cycleway has to bypass this by climbing the hillside on the left. A view therefrom shows the depot in the foreground with the still-standing Carlyon Farm chimney stacks rising from the heavily wooded valley. *Bernard Mills/DHM*

LOWER RUDDLE YARD: The rest of the branch opened on 24 May 1920. About three-quarters of a mile beyond Bojea there was a reverse siding leading to a loading dock, served by rails on each side. No 4552 is on the left-hand road in June 1958, with the running line visible in front of the loco. The wagons on a higher level to the left are in Boskell Sidings. Instructions for working Lower Ruddle were: 'The junction is on a gradient of 1 in 40, rising towards Lansalson. The two sidings will each berth about 13 wagons in position for loading, and in the berthing of wagons care must be taken to see the roadway over the lines is left clear. Wagons for or from this Yard must only be negotiated by trains from the Trenance Junction end. When trains from Trenance Junction require to do work at Lower Ruddle, the engine of such trains must not be detached until the Guard has securely applied the van brake, sprigged the wheels and pinned down sufficient brakes on the wagons next to the van to an extent such as will establish a safeguard against any receding of the wagons that may have to be left on the Running line.

Wagons requiring to be picked up in Lower Ruddle must be taken to and placed in Boskell Siding, and eventually be cleared by Up trains. When such wagons are being taken from Lower Ruddle to Boskell, the Shunter must place himself in a position to be able to operate the hand brake on the rearmost wagon in case of emergency. Trains must not work at Lower Ruddle during the hours of darkness.'

A rough track now follows this part of the branch and runs over the loading dock; the 'present' view is looking down the ramp, with the siding area on both sides overgrown. *Norman Simmons/DHM*

LOWER LANSALSON: There were no restrictions on engines that could be used on this branch, but in practice it was one of St Blazey's '57XX' pannier tanks or '45XX' 'Prairie' tanks that worked the usual daily trip in later steam years, with 350hp diesel shunters taking over in either late 1961 or early 1962. On 11 May 1968 the Plymouth Railway Circle's 'The Clayliner' tour has reached the limit of its journey. It is on the section retained as a headshunt for Lower Ruddle and Boskell sidings when the final quarter-mile of the branch was closed in July 1964. 'Bubble car' No W55016 is probably the last train to traverse these rails, as the branch had closed five days earlier. Other interesting locations visited by this tour earlier that day included Moorswater, Pinnock Tunnel, Meledor Mill, East Caudledown, Carbis Wharf and Parkandillack.

The rails were lifted in 1969. Today a branch off the cycleway bridges the B3374 road to the left, and continues to Ruddlemoor behind the camera; part of the formation has been built up to give access to this bridge. All the 'present' photos on this branch were taken on 18 September 2008. *Bernard Mills/DHM*

LANSALSON: An earlier PRC railtour, the 'Cornwall Mineral' special of 28 April 1962, is being propelled by Nos 5531 and 4564 towards the terminus in Lansalson yard, a mere 1 mile 53 chains from Trenance Junction. The engines had hauled the train to Bojea, where they had run round the 11 brake-vans and propelled them the rest of the way; there being no run-round facilities at Lansalson. The special is running into the left of two roads, with the public loading wharf visible at the rear of the train. This was the final steam working from St Blazey shed and will be seen at three further locations in this book. The houses are part of Ruddlemoor village.

The same view today is obscured by tree growth, but in this track-level view of the yard some surviving rails can be seen embedded in a road that leads to Lansalson Farm. The wharf was demolished during May 1989. The houses provide a further link with the 'past' photo and, by following the road north past them for less than a mile, the explorer will arrive at Carbean, the site of the terminus of another mineral branch (see *British Railways Past & Present No 54*). *Peter W. Gray/DHM*

Burngullow to St Dennis Junction

CRUGWALLINS: The broad-gauge Newquay & Cornwall Junction Railway was promoted with the aim of connecting the Cornwall Railway at Burngullow with Treffry's tramway from Newquay to Hendra, serving a number of clay pits en route. Opening on 1 July 1869, the line leaves Burngullow Junction on a steeply graded curve before shortly passing the site of Burngullow West Siding, then reaching Crugwallins Siding, only 17 chains from the junction. This siding was opened by English China Clays in 1907 to serve a kiln, with the works later used to house Burngullow tube press (names hereabouts can be confusing!). Nos 37142 and 25207 are passing with a train from Drinnick Mill to St Blazey on 29 September 1978.

Latterly the works was provided with its own shunter, and activity continued intermittently until clay-drying ceased after 100 years in 2007; the final train to remove stocks left in October that year. The overgrown 'present' photo was taken in November 2008. *Both DHM*

CARPELLA: In 1907 the GWR became embroiled in a dispute with the Carpella United China Clay Co over mineral rights. The latter wished to extract clay from beneath the railway and in due course the House of Lords ruled that china clay was indeed a mineral, and a quarter-mile section of line was closed in December 1909. Eventually on 18 April 1922 a deviation was opened that crossed the old trackbed just beyond High Street Siding and skirted the east side of Carpella pit before rejoining the original formation near Carpella Siding. Recorded from an occupation bridge, 0-6-0PTs Nos 9755 and 1624 are descending from Drinnick Mill on this 'new' section on the afternoon of 13 July 1961; the close proximity of the clay pit can be seen on the left. At the front of the train are three empty wagons that will be shunted into New Carpella Siding. The village of Carpalla is in view – note the different spelling (see also page 6).

On 30 May 2006 English Electric Type 3 No 37411 tails Standard Class 4MT 2-6-0 No 76079 on the 'China Clay Pony' tour. *Peter W. Gray/DHM*

39

DRINNICK MILL JUNCTION: Although promoted with the aim of linking with Treffry's horse-drawn tramway near St Dennis, the N&CJR ran out of funds and only managed to reach Drinnick Mill, partly due to the cost of a long cutting blasted through granite near Nanpean. Eventually the Cornwall Minerals Railway purchased and rebuilt the tramway in 1874, extending its standard gauge track to Drinnick. The CMR also took over the N&CJR, but there was to be a break of gauge between the two lines here until the broad gauge was abolished in 1892. No 47343 is on the main running line, having arrived with a train from the Parkandillack direction on 25 April 1985; the original N&CJR route is descending to Nanpean Wharf on the right. The loco is next to the control building that was the administrative centre for wagon movements in the area, and also contained a crew rest room. Although Drinnick Mill has never had a proper station, it was deemed important enough to have a station master in earlier times.

The building was demolished in October 1993 and the site of the junction is viewed in September 2007.
James Besley/DHM

Continuing financial problems in the line's early years led to all of the 47 miles of line owned by the CMR being worked by the GWR from 1 October 1877, with full amalgamation from 1 July 1896. Looking in the opposite direction on 1 October 1955, No 4526 is standing on the junction while taking water. It is working a Plymouth Railway Circle special comprising six ex-GWR 'Toad' brake-vans. The rails of Dubbers No 2 Siding can be glimpsed on the left. At one time no fewer than 26 sidings were in use in the 7 miles from Burngullow to St Dennis Junction. *Peter W. Gray*

A little further north in July 1960, No 9655 pauses next to Drinnick Mill's small signal cabin. With grades of up to 1 in 37, curves of up to 18-chain radius and tight clearances to negotiate in some of the sidings, there were restrictions on the steam locos that could traverse this route and only 'Uncoloured' and 'Yellow' engines (ie with an axle load up to 16 tons) were authorised. Effectively this meant that pannier tanks dominated workings on the whole route from Burngullow to St Dennis Junction, much of which was subject to a 10mph speed limit. *Hugh Davies*

41

NANPEAN WHARF: The 3-mile 10-chain broad-gauge N&CJR terminated here, the line dropping from Drinnick Mill Junction at a gradient of 1 in 50. Also known in the past as Drinnick Mill Goods, this was a public goods station comprising two sidings, with a trailing connection that ran back beneath the main branch to the Drinnick low-level lines. A four-coach opening day special was one of the few passenger trains ever to reach Nanpean; more than 100 years later one of the last to do so was a DMU tour on 13 November 1983.

China clay and other traffic was handled here, but by 1988 it was reported that the wharf was only used for some general merchandise, comprising small amounts of fruit outwards, and explosives inwards. The last type of freight to be handled was calcified seaweed in the early 1990s. This product was used as a fertiliser, but dredging off the Cornish coast has since ceased, as harvesting the seaweed is no longer considered to be sustainable due to adverse effects on the marine environment. By 22 April 1997 the location was disused other than for the storage of redundant four-wheel clay slurry tank wagons that were waiting to be scrapped.

The wharf is now heavily overgrown, as recorded on 20 September 2007. Although rails are still embedded in the adjacent occupation crossing, the warning sign is superfluous, as the track to the junction with the main branch has been lifted. *Nigel Tregoning/DHM (2)*

Another view from 13 November 1983 illustrates that the loading platform was rather on the high side for passenger traffic! During the mid-1980s the railways of Cornwall enjoyed a brief period of relative autonomy under the Truro Area Manager, and this branch-line tour was organised during this regime. *Ian Cavill*

DRINNICK LOW LEVEL: This line dropped below the main branch on a falling gradient, initially at about 1 in 40, and was just under half a mile long. Originally serving the Carloggos, Barne and North Carloggos china clay kilns, latterly the track layout basically comprised three overlapping loops serving Drinnick Nos 1-8 dryers. There was also a coal-fired power station, built in 1936 to serve the clay industry. Clay loading ceased in the early 1980s and for a couple of years the only traffic was domestic coal to a distribution depot established adjacent to the closed power station. Subsequently there was a revival in clay traffic, but only spasmodically, and the last loaded Polybulk wagon departed from Drinnick No 7 in May 1992, with a Ferrywagon loaded at Drinnick No 6 in December of that year. Owing to the increased cost of track repairs and ECC's reluctance to meet this expense, the lines below the former power station siding were clipped out of use on 13 February 1993. The bottom end of the complex is seen in September 1994, with Drinnick No 7 on the left, and other kilns on the right; the old chimney stack belonged to the long closed North Carloggos works.

Much of the site has been cleared but part of the stack is just visible in September 2007, with surviving track set in concrete. Plans were published in 2008 to redevelop the site as a business park. *Both DHM*

DRINNICK MILL: Back on what was officially known as the Cornwall Junction branch, No 3635 stands next to Drinnick Mill's 1921-vintage signal cabin on 20 June 1956, before departing with the 10.50am goods to Burngullow. The stonework to the left of the rear of the train is the bridge over the low-level line. Considerable care had to be taken in working this line, as illustrated by the events of 9 June 1952 when No 8733 was hauling 22 clay wagons and a brake-van and was unable to halt at the stop board about half a mile below Drinnick, the engine's wheels locking due to the greasy state of the rails. The train's speed was only 5mph, but the brakes on the van could not be applied as it is understood that the guard was travelling on the footplate, and although he leapt off he was unable to rejoin his van. The train careered onwards, crashing through Lanjeth's level crossing gates and eventually colliding with stationary No 4568 at Burngullow. The train's fireman and the crew on the 'Prairie' jumped clear, but the driver stayed at the regulator and unfortunately later succumbed to his injuries.

The signal box was located just north of the control office, but closed in 1966 when the line beyond Parkandillack was taken out of use; the whole branch then came under the control of Burngullow box. No 47343 is seen again on 25 April 1985. *Hugh Davies/James Besley*

RESTOWRACK SIDING: China clay (or kaolin) is decomposed granite where the feldspar crystals have changed to a fine white clay, leaving the quartz and mica in the rock unchanged. Also found in this area is china stone, a granite that has only been partially altered by the process of kaolinisation, and is quarried like other rock. This siding belonged to the Goonvean & Rostowrack company (an independent producer that still trades today), and was in use from 1923 to load china stone. Viewed from Slip bridge, less than a mile from Drinnick, No 25207 is in the middle of a shunting move on 29 September 1978. Until 1965 a siding had trailed off the main branch in the left foreground serving Slip Quarry, an important source of china stone.

Traffic from Restowrack Siding was intermittent in later years and ceased in 1984, with the siding lifted and pointwork replaced by plain track in November 1990. No 37406 tails 'Black 5' No 45407 on the 1228 Plymouth to Parkandillack 'China Clay Pony' charter on 28 March 2007. The line's summit is just east of here and it is now downhill all the way. *Both DHM*

KERNICK SIDING: 'Prairie' tanks Nos 5531 and 4564 are seen again with the PRC's 'Cornwall Mineral' special on Saturday 28 April 1962. Kernick Dryer is on the right with its siding set in concrete. Both the branch and siding curve away to the right, where the latter also serves the Treviscoe and Central Treviscoe loading areas. From 1913 to 1950 there was a signal box on the left of the running line, positioned approximately adjacent to the rear of this train. The present end of the line at Parkandillack is just over a mile from here, and 5 miles 26 chains from Burngullow. The current terminus is another location with spelling alternatives; the railway always prefers this version, whereas the clay companies seem to usually prefer Parkandillick.

The inevitable undergrowth meant that a more head-on stance had to be adopted to record No 66078 on its way to Burngullow with traffic from Central Treviscoe on 18 November 2008; the Kernick/Treviscoe complex and Parkandillack are now the only loading points on this branch. *Peter F. Bowles/DHM*

47

ST DENNIS JUNCTION: Rails first reached this location when Treffry's horse-drawn standard-gauge tramway was constructed to link Newquay Harbour with the developing china clay industry in the St Dennis area. Although an opening date of 1849 is usually quoted, recent research suggests that this line was not fully operational until 1857. The Cornwall Minerals Railway took over the operation and opened its own steam-operated line from Newquay to Fowey on 1 June 1874, when this location was known as Bodmin Road Junction. Branches were also opened at that time from here to Drinnick Mill (an extension of the original tramway from Whitegates, near St Dennis) and Melangoose Mill. This site was given its later name in 1878. On 1 October 1955 0-6-0PT No 3705 pulls into the yard with a train from the Retew branch, as 2-6-2T No 4526 runs round the PRC special previously seen at Drinnick Mill Junction; it will then take the tour down to Meledor Mill.

The line from here to Parkandillack was closed on 6 February 1966, with the Retew branch to Meledor Mill being officially closed on 3 April 1982. Some track in the yard was initially used to serve a spoil tip, but the remaining sidings were disconnected from the Newquay branch in February 1992. The yard area is now disused; the furrows in the foreground in November 2008 are timber sleepers slowly rotting in situ, while the route of the Retew branch can be noted to the right. *Peter W Gray/DHM*

ST DENNIS JUNCTION: Looking in the opposite direction in June 1958, No 9755 is adjacent to the 40-lever signal box as it runs round a train of clay empties from St Blazey. It will then take the Drinnick Mill route and, after shunting various locations, will head for home via Burngullow. Meanwhile a 'Prairie' tank hauls its Par to Newquay service at a maximum of 15mph on the sharp curve in front of the box. There is double track for almost 2 miles to the right, but the main branch becomes single again just the other side of the A30 overbridge.

The double-track section was singled in 1965, leaving a passing loop that continued in use until the box closed on 14 December 1986. The same view today is one of bushes, and palisade fencing runs alongside the remaining single track, with a 'new' A30 bridge overhead. An alternative view from the site of the recently demolished signal box on 4 October 1987 includes 'Skipper' No 142025 approaching as the 1326 service from Newquay to Par. Other views of this location can be seen in the East Cornwall volume. *Norman Simmons/DHM*

Retew branch

MELANGOOSE MILL: This branch initially ran for just over 2½ miles from St Dennis Junction to Melangoose Mill in the Fal valley, near the hamlet of Retew. In this view of the original terminus looking north, the roof of the large Anchor works is in the foreground with a public loading wharf visible immediately above it. Beyond this is the Wheal Benallick works and siding with its large clay settling tanks at the rear of the linhays. Dropping away at 1 in 40 in the right foreground is the extension of the branch, just over a mile long, that was opened to Meledor Mill by the GWR on 1 July 1912. This photo dates from before 1925 when a loop siding was added adjacent to this extension. *Author's collection*

VIRGINIA CROSSING: Just north of Tolbenny Siding, 2-6-2T No 5519 is approaching this occupation crossing with a loaded train from Meledor Mill on 19 June 1958. After passing over the gated crossing, the train will also soon cross the River Fal, which is little more than a stream at this point. Kernick Siding on the Cornwall Junction branch is only about half a mile east of here 'as the crow flies'. *Norman Simmons*

MELEDOR MILL: Much of the route of this branch has been obliterated, both by nature and extended clay workings, involving the movement of a great deal of spoil and waste. The trackbed is largely inaccessible today and a selection of 'past' views is included to give a flavour of a fascinating byway that was rarely visited by photographers.

Only 'Uncoloured' engines were permitted over this line, but 'Yellow' '45XX'/'55XX' 'Prairie' tanks and 'Blue' '57XX' pannier tanks were specially authorised, and in practice it was these two types that operated in later steam years, with up to three trains a day timetabled to service the many sidings at a maximum speed of 15mph. There was no signalling, and the branch was operated on a 'One engine in steam' basis. No 4526 is near the end of the line with the PRC special of 1 October 1955. *Peter W. Gray*

MELEDOR LOOP SOUTH GROUND FRAME: Although the branch was dieselised by early 1962, the author is yet to see a photo of a diesel-hauled clay train on this line. The last of a handful of railtours to traverse the route was the Lea Valley Railway Club's 'The Royal Duchy' on 30 April 1977, which comprised Metro-Cammell DMUs Nos B800/802. It is pictured at the extent of its journey, with the Meledor Mill platforms a short distance behind the photographer. *Ian Cavill*

MELEDOR MILL: This was a public goods station with two lengthy loading platforms. The empty clay wagon is standing next to a single-face platform on the left, while Nos 4564 and 5531 are at the other double-sided wharf in our third view of the PRC's 'Cornwall Mineral' special of 28 April 1962. This tour had nearly 100 participants riding in 11 brake-vans. Starting in Truro, it ran first to Newham, then to Chacewater, where the line to Newquay was taken as far as Tolcarn Junction. There the little-used spur was used to reach the Par line, and this was traversed as far as Bugle for a visit to the Carbis Wharf branch. After returning to St Dennis Junction and making the journey to Meledor Mill, the special headed for St Austell via Burngullow. After reaching Lansalson, the tank engines set out for Par, where most of the passengers detrained. After a final reversal, the special terminated at St Blazey's closed station. One only wishes that this itinerary could be repeated today!

This branch served almost 20 sidings at the height of its activity, but most of these were officially closed in the 1966-73 period, with the likelihood that many hadn't seen any use in years. The old coal-fired clay works were gradually closed and, as working methods were modernised, particularly with improved pipeline technology, traffic dwindled and was sporadic during the 1970s. Although much of this site is overgrown, a rough road runs beside one of the platforms. *Peter W. Gray/DHM*

MELEDOR LEVEL CROSSING On 11 October 1921 a further extension was opened beyond the public siding and, after passing over a level crossing, the rails finally ended at New Meledor (or Collins) Siding. The Sectional Appendix advised that this crossing was 'Situated at 4 miles 0 chains, near the termination of Branch. When it is necessary to work the Cornish Meledor China Clay Co's Siding after dark, the Shunter must first obtain the gate lamp, which is kept in a locked box at the crossing, light it, and place it on the north gate. After closing the gates across the roadway, he may hand signal the train over the crossing. The Shunter must replace the gates across the line, remove the lamp and replace it in the box on completion of the work. Enginemen must keep a sharp look-out and sound their whistles when approaching any of the level crossings on the Branch.'

It is believed that the final clay train on this branch departed from 'Collins' in September 1980, and that the weedkilling train visited it in the summer of 1981! In March 1982 a loco and van worked to the end of the branch, just before it was 'officially' closed when removed from the Sectional Appendix in a notice dated 3 April 1982. Most of the track had been lifted by May 1983, but the decaying north gate could still be viewed on 20 September 1992. This has now been removed, but a buffer stop at the end of a short stub siding remains in situ in 2008. Just beyond this, the original wrought-iron posts survive from the entrance to the goods station, though these have been repositioned. *Both DHM*

Routes to Newquay

ST DENNIS JUNCTION: Certain St Blazey diagrams changed from steam to diesel-hydraulic from 11 May 1960, and in consequence a number of Par to Newquay trains were thereafter diesel-hauled. North British Type 2 No D6312 approaches the A30 road bridge with a train from Newquay at 11.20am on Sunday 6 August 1961. On the left a short platform serves as a base for a wooden signal post, corrugated iron hut and water tower.

All three lineside accoutrements had disappeared by 29 September 1978, but the track layout is unaltered; the 1144 from Par is leaving the passing loop as it heads for Newquay.

On 18 November 2008 No 150233 approaches forming the 1259 Newquay to Par service. *R. A. Lumber/DHM (2)*

QUINTREL DOWNS: The CMR's route from St Dennis Junction initially followed the formation of the original tramway to St Columb Road station, but after less than half a mile there is a deviation. Treffry's line had included the damp and low 530-yard-long Toldish Tunnel, but the new railway bypassed this by taking a longer route to the north. Quintrel Downs was once the site of a passing loop and siding, complete with a signal box. Subsequently the layout was altered to a single running line with two sidings, and a platform was erected, the station opening from 2 October 1911. The signal box was closed at that time, with the sidings controlled from a ground frame. The station is located immediately next to the A392 road, but the level crossing is just out of sight to the right of this view. The suffix 'Platform' was used here until 1956.

The sidings were taken out of use in 1965, but the station is still open. The railway traditionally used one 'l' in the station name, but for at least 20 years the platform nameboard has read 'Quintrell Downs', thus conforming to the spelling of the adjacent community. Timetables have followed suit since 2002. *Lens of Sutton Association/DHM*

NEWQUAY: Treffry's tramway crossed the Trenance Valley, just outside Newquay, by means of a spindly viaduct of largely timber construction. The CMR replaced this with a new structure comprising iron girders on stone piers, but this in turn was replaced by the GWR in 1938 with a double-track masonry viaduct, although the second track did not come into use until 20 March 1946. On this date a new signal box was opened at the end of the long island platform, the third such installation to be located within the station area. 'Prairie' tank No 4588 has just crossed the 154-yard-long viaduct and is passing the 45-lever box as it arrives in Platform 1 in June 1958. The engine was based at Truro, which suggests that the train is probably from Chacewater.

Viewed from Platform 2 on 29 August 1987, the signalman is about to receive the token from the driver of No 50044 *Exeter* as it arrives with the 0723 train from Manchester.

Only the former Platform 2 is used today, and No 150239 is leaving as the 1259 service to Par on 29 September 2008. *Norman Simmons/R A Lumber/DHM*

Newquay signal box is seen on its last day of use, Sunday 4 October 1987, with two surviving carriage sidings in the foreground. The last scheduled locomotive-hauled train had departed the previous day, at the end of the Summer timetable, and only a single line and platform will be in use from the next day. The box was subsequently used by permanent way workers, but was burned down in 1997. The Newquay branch is now operated as two block sections with operational signal boxes at St Blazey and Goonbarrow Junction, each having token instruments. Goonbarrow Junction has a loop, so can pass Newquay line trains. Additionally a china clay train can be locked in the sidings there. *DHM*

NEWQUAY station was opened by the CMR for goods traffic from June 1874, with the first passenger train arriving at its single platform on 20 June 1876. The Great Western rebuilt the station in 1904-06 for the opening of the Chacewater line, with the original platform extended and an island one added. The GWR was instrumental in developing the town as a holiday resort and improvements to cater for the increase in traffic included further extensions to Platform 1 in 1928 and 1934, with the island platform lengthened in 1938. 4-6-0 No 7816 *Frilsham Manor* has arrived in the original platform with the 1222pm train from Par on 12 June 1958 and is about to use the engine release crossover. The town gasworks is in the background. An engine shed and turntable were provided here until about 1930, but the site was then used for additional carriage sidings and subsequently locomotives were turned by using the triangle at Tolcarn Junction, about half a mile beyond Trenance Viaduct.

The island platform's canopy was greatly reduced in 1964, as seen on a wet 3 May 1969, shortly before the DMU departed as the 1320 service to Bodmin Road.

The remaining single track and platform have been truncated, with the buffer stops positioned beyond the short section of protective canopy. The awning on the closed Platform 1 has also been reduced to match it, with the buildings demolished. The third view is from 21 March 1992 and shows the rare visit of Nos 33050 *Isle of Grain* and 33063, which have arrived with the 'Cornish Construction Crompton' railtour. A seagull stands on the basic glass shelter then provided on the platform.

The final view on 29 September 2008 is from a little further to the north and includes a glimpse of the shortened awning. The station has been tidied up and No 150239 stands next to an attractive, but tiny, replacement shelter. Palm trees provide an exotic touch on the former Platform 1. *P. K. Tunks/R. A. Lumber/ DHM (2)*

59

NEWQUAY HARBOUR: The small existing harbour was rebuilt to cater for a burgeoning trade and to provide better shelter from the often wild Atlantic, the work being completed by 1833. It was acquired by J. T. Treffry in 1838 and he built a tramway from the south quay to a location that would eventually become Newquay station. To reach the town on the top of a cliff the line climbed at an average 1 in 4½ through an 80-yards tunnel. A horse-powered winch and rope was used to haul wagons up the incline, but this was soon replaced by stationary steam engines. This postcard (sent in 1912) shows rails on both the south quay and the central jetty (built by the CMR in 1872-73). Wagon movements around the harbour were horse-powered. Traffic to the quays included iron ore and china clay, but this had dwindled by the end of the 19th century, particularly as larger modern ships were unable to use the tidal harbour.

The last outbound shipload that involved use of the tramway was in 1921, with an inbound load of fertiliser in the following year. The wooden trestle that connected the central stone jetty to land was demolished in the 1950s. The harbour is still home to a small fishing fleet, with pleasure craft catering for the tourist industry. *Author's collection/DHM*

MITCHELL & NEWLYN HALT: The Newquay to Chacewater line was constructed in several parts, with the section from Tolcarn Junction to near the village of St Newlyn East originally forming a branch to Treffry's tramway. This opened in 1849 to transport lead and silver ore from East Wheal Rose mine. After being acquired by the CMR, the railway was extended to Treamble. Finally, on 2 January 1905 this section was opened to passengers when the Chacewater to Perranporth branch was extended to Newquay by the GWR. This was one of six halts opened on this line on 14 August 1905. Originally a timber structure erected on the east side of a bridge over a road leading to the villages of Mitchell (nearly 2½ miles to the south-east) and St Newlyn East (less than a mile to the north), the halt was subsequently rebuilt on the other side of the bridge and provided with a 100-foot-long concrete platform and a very basic corrugated iron shelter.

The road bridge has been taken out, but the platform and shelter are still remarkably intact, though are being gradually overwhelmed by flora. *Author's collection/DHM*

GOONHAVERN HALT: Although there was earlier habitation, the organised hamlet did not appear until the age of industrialised mining in the early 1800s. It was located at an important crossroads and on rising ground between the coast and high central spine of Cornwall. By the mid-19th century it comprised about 20 dwellings, but by the end of that century it had grown to include a school and Wesleyan Chapel. The railway was built through the village in a cutting, passing under three roads, including the main one from Newquay to Redruth. The halt was erected next to what became the B3285 from Perranporth. The original timber platform was subsequently rebuilt, with a brick facing to the base.

Since closure the site of the halt has been obliterated with the cutting filled in and the road widened. This and the next six 'present' photos were taken on 9 October 2008. *Author's collection/DHM*

PERRANPORTH: This was one of the two most important intermediate settlements served by this line. The town's ancient name is Perranzabuloe, which is still the name of the parish, and mining once dominated its life. Although tin, iron, lead, zinc and silver were all brought out in the area, the prosperity of the town came largely from two giant copper mines. Wheal Leisure and Perran Great St George were an amalgam of five smaller mines with their heyday in the middle of the 19th century. These mines were not good neighbours and in 1870, after years of dispute, the owners of Wheal Leisure sued their rivals for encroaching into their lodes. The courts found in their favour, but in retaliation the other mine ceased to operate and closed down its pumps, thus flooding both operations and effectively ruining the local copper industry. Today many miles of galleries and tunnels lie beneath the town. Our final view of the PRC's 28 April 1962 tour finds Nos 5531 and 4564 pausing next to the island platform with the large goods shed on the left; rather unusually for Cornwall, access to the platform was gained via a subway. The 23-lever signal box was mounted on the platform and can be noted above the engines.

Today a small industrial estate covers the site of the station. *Terry Nicholls/DHM*

63

PERRANPORTH BEACH HALT: The town today is famous for its magnificent beach, nearly 3 miles long and consisting almost entirely of pure sand. From at least 1800 it was fashionable for Truro people to visit the beach, and from the middle of that century tourists from further afield began visiting the town. By 1876 sea bathing was so popular that it was decreed that the western part of the beach was reserved for men up to 9.00am, with exclusive use by ladies from then until 12 noon. The opening of the branch line from Chacewater on 6 July 1903 allowed many more the opportunity to visit Perranporth, and did much to encourage its growth as a resort. By 1931 business was sufficient for the Great Western management to authorise the construction of this halt, nearer the beach and town centre than the main station, at an estimated cost of £720. Facilities included a booking office, staffed during summer months, and a waiting room. In 1949 the platform and buildings were renewed in concrete at an estimated cost of £2,200, with electric lighting also installed.

After closure, sections of the platform were used in the building of a new station in Falmouth. When visited in 2008, the site was showing early signs of redevelopment, but access could be gained by using the original footpath and gate. In the distance housing has been built across the formation, but beyond this a bridge abutment survives, with a footpath on the trackbed. Behind the camera a deep overgrown cutting curves away towards the site of the main station. *Lens of Sutton Association/DHM*

MITHIAN HALT: From Perranporth the line climbed at up to 1 in 45 for just over 2 miles along the Perrancombe Valley to reach this halt, which was close to the hamlet it served. Located in a deep cutting, the original timber platform had been replaced with a more substantial 102-foot-long structure by 1922. Four of the halts opened on this line in August 1905 were provided with the distinctive corrugated 'Pagoda' waiting shelters. These were assembled on site from parts, the sides were bolted together to form an open box, then the roof would be constructed at ground level before being lifted into position by a gang of men.

Since closure, all evidence of this halt has disappeared with the cutting filled in and the road bridge removed, although one side of the next bridge to the north does survive. Rather than include a view of a field, another 'past' scene has 'Prairie' tank No 4593 with the 4.25pm Truro to Newquay train near the halt on 9 July 1960. *Lens of Sutton Association/Peter W. Gray*

GOONBELL VIADUCT: About a mile further on the rails crossed the most notable structure on the line, a 140-yard-long five-arch viaduct of stone construction. 0-6-0PT No 9635 is crossing with the 11.40am Truro to Newquay train on 11 July 1961. After the use of steam railmotors in the early days, 'Metro' 2-4-0Ts provided the usual motive power on this route until '45XX' 2-6-2Ts achieved pre-eminence in the 1930s, supplemented on occasions by pannier tanks. 'Manor' 4-6-0s and '43XX' 'Moguls' were permitted in an emergency, but at a maximum speed of 20mph, the line otherwise having a speed limit of 40mph. In the 1950s through trains operated between Perranporth and Paddington on summer Saturdays, but these ran as a 'Prairie' tank-hauled six-coach service to Truro, where additional coaches were added and a 4-6-0 provided for the onward journey. Diesel multiple units and North British Type 2 diesel-hydraulics took over for the last few months of the line's existence.

The viaduct survives today, but inevitable growth dictated that the 2008 photo be taken from a different angle to gain a clearer view. *Peter W. Gray/DHM*

GOONBELL HALT: Easy access from public roads was of prime consideration when selecting sites for the halts on this line. Viewed from a road bridge, this halt was also in a deep cutting, and adjacent to the hamlet of Goonbell, just south-east of St Agnes; the halt was slightly closer to St Agnes than that village's own station.

This 17-mile-long line was the last passenger branch to open in Cornwall, and the first to close completely to all traffic. The final trains ran on 2 February 1963, this part of the branch having had a life of just under 60 years. Apparently the decaying platform and shelter survived here for a further 15 years or so, but the cutting was subsequently infilled. A parapet from the overbridge survives, but the view therefrom is somewhat less than inspiring! *Lens of Sutton Association/DHM*

ST AGNES was the only intermediate station when the original branch was opened to Perranporth on 6 July 1903, sited about a mile south of the mining village it purported to serve. It originally had a single platform, which was located on a curve adjacent to the main station building. The station was rebuilt in 1937 when a 300-foot-long island platform, footbridge and 30-lever signal box were provided, and it became one of three crossing places on the line (the others being Perranporth and Shepherds). In this undated view from a road bridge (Goonbell Halt is only about a mile down this road), the station building is on the right, with the loop running over the site of the original platform. The GWR's first camping coaches were available for occupancy from Easter 1934, and St Agnes was one of the initial sites; two such vehicles can be seen near the platform.

Most of the site was cleared after closure, but the station building survived and is now used by a light engineering firm. It is obscured, however, in another view from the still standing bridge, as a garden now covers the foreground area. *Lens of Sutton Association/DHM*

MOUNT HAWKE HALT, complete with its 100-foot-long brick-faced platform, was sited in a chalk cutting about a mile to the east of its namesake village. 'Prairie' tank No 5562 runs into the empty platform with the 4.35pm service from Newquay to Truro at 5.30pm on Monday 10 July 1961. After just over a mile the train will come alongside the main line near the erstwhile Blackwater Junction East. When the line opened this was a triangular junction with three signal boxes, but the little-used west loop was taken out of use on 5 May 1919. The boxes remained active until 9 November 1924, when branch trains started using an independent third track into Chacewater station.

Passenger loadings held up well on this line and actually increased during the 1950s, but the fact that there was an alternative route to Newquay no doubt contributed to its early closure. However, in many ways this line was of greater local value as most trains ran through to the county town, with connections to the nearby Redruth and Camborne conurbation from Chacewater. After closure the platform remained until the cutting was infilled in 1982. Surviving railway fencing on the right is the best link between the two scenes. *Peter W. Gray/DHM*

Truro to Falmouth

Below: HIGHERTOWN TUNNEL, 70 yards long, was dug by the broad-gauge Cornwall Railway and opened in 1859 to provide a connection between its Truro station and the standard-gauge West Cornwall Railway at Penwithers Junction. The latter had opened its extension from Redruth to a temporary station known as Truro Road, at Highertown, on 25 August 1852, but this was replaced on 16 April 1855 when its line was further extended to a new terminus at Newham. The West Cornwall gained running powers through the tunnel, which initially had two single lines of the different gauges. The CR opened its broad-gauge 11¾-mile branch line to Falmouth on 24 August 1863. The West Cornwall was obliged by law to provide access for broad-gauge trains over its route to Penzance and the CR gave notice of a requirement to do this in 1864, thus putting an end to the operational problems and inconvenience caused by the break of gauge. Mixed-gauge goods train operation finally started on 6 November 1866, with passenger services following from 1 March 1867. However, the left-hand road through the tunnel was used solely by main-line services with the other reserved for Falmouth trains. 'Prairie' tanks Nos 5509 and 5552 emerge from the tunnel with the 6.00pm Truro to Falmouth service on Whit Monday, 6 June 1960.

A 'present' view is omitted as it was not possible to obtain a satisfactory photo in 2008, due to the overgrowth. *Derek Frost*

Opposite: PENWITHERS JUNCTION: A few minutes earlier the photographer had pointed his camera in the opposite direction to record 0-6-0PT No 4622 and the 5.24pm Falmouth to Truro service. The train has just passed to the left of the 36-lever signal box; the main line to Penzance curves away to the right, while the Newham branch can be glimpsed trailing in from the left beyond the train. A loop was provided at the junction that allowed Newham trains to run round, there never being a direct connection from Truro. The Newham line originally crossed the Falmouth route on the level before a connection was established with the main line. The track layout was altered and realigned by early 1894 when the main line was doubled, and the signal box was erected to replace an earlier structure.

The junction was rationalised from 7 November 1971 when the Newham branch was taken out of use and the signal box closed. There is no longer any connection between the two main running lines, with two-way running for Falmouth services over the down main to Truro station. *Derek Frost*

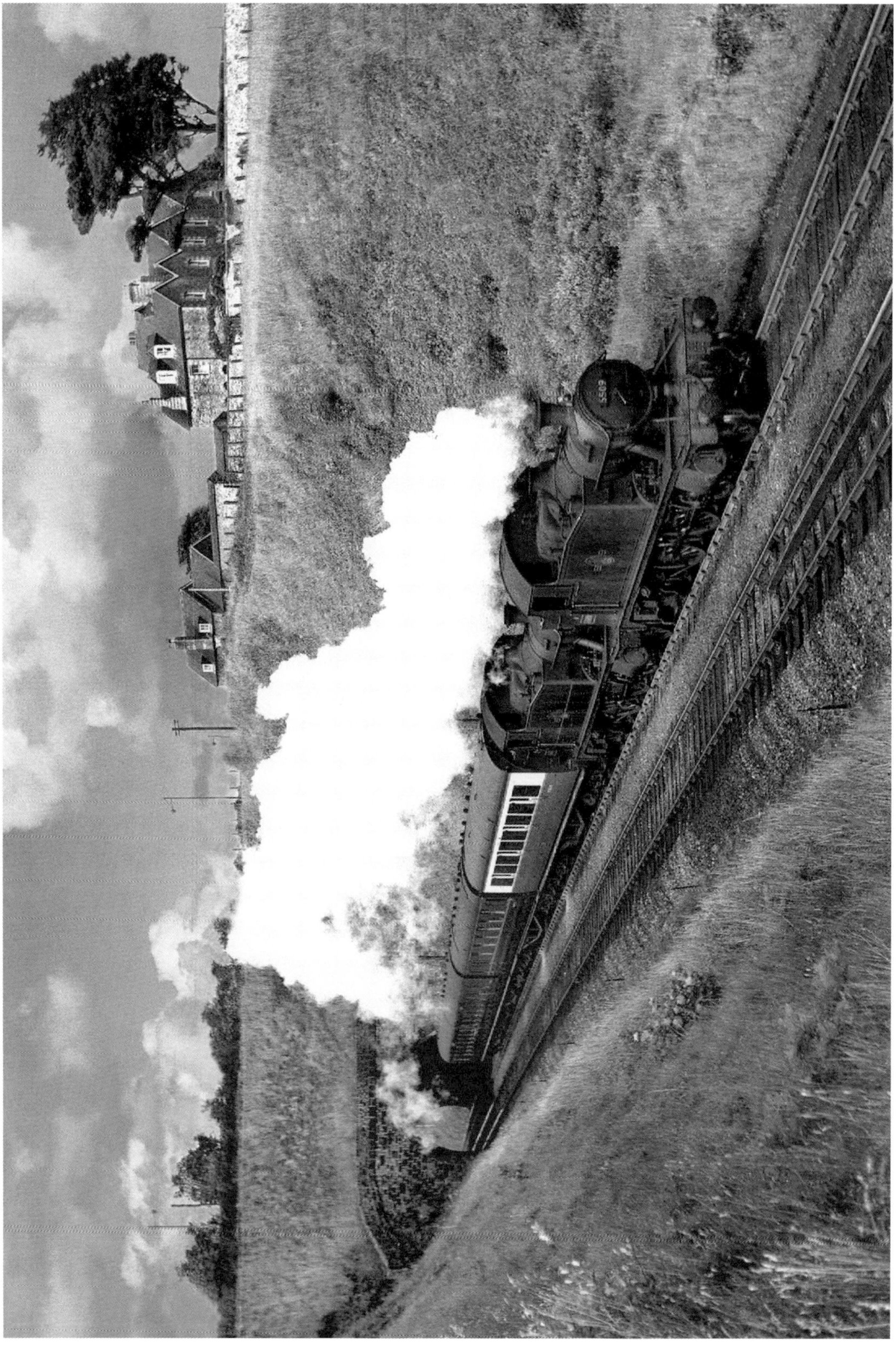

NEWHAM: For four years this terminus on the west bank of the Truro River was the town's sole station, but with the arrival of the Cornwall Railway most trains were diverted to its station, and passenger services to here finally ceased from 16 September 1863. The line, almost 2½ miles long, was then only used for goods traffic. However, the old wooden train shed, complete with its overall roof, remarkably survived for a further 100 years or so. With its location on the quayside close to the town centre, Newham was handily placed and for many years dealt with about a half of all goods traffic handled in Truro, with domestic coal an important source of revenue. A siding was provided for a nearby gasworks in 1955. For much of its history the branch was served by two trains each weekday, but only one ran on Saturdays. Pannier tank No 7422 was recorded on 14 August 1956 – this was the usual branch engine at this time.

The gasworks siding was in use until 1970, and the line closed from 8 November 1971. A road now runs through the site with commercial development on both sides; a cycleway follows the route of the branch towards Penwithers Junction. *Hugh Davies/DHM*

PERRANWELL: In the 3½ miles from Penwithers Junction, the Falmouth branch as built crossed three of Brunel's timber viaducts and passed through the 491-yard-long Sparnick Tunnel before reaching this station, thus providing an indication of the heavy engineering that was required in constructing the line. Two of these viaducts were eventually replaced by embankments, while the third, named Carnon and less than half a mile from Perranwell, carried the branch over the 1826 4-foot-gauge Redruth & Chasewater mineral railway. This was one of the last timber viaducts in Cornwall to be rebuilt, its replacement opening in 1933. 'Prairie' tank No 4588 enters one of the two original intermediate stations with a train from Falmouth in the 1950s.

The crossing loop was taken out of use and the signal box closed on 18 April 1966, leaving the former down platform in use. A pair of single units, Nos 153329 and 153318, approach forming the 1654 Falmouth Docks to Truro service on 25 September 2008. With the introduction of two-train operation in May 2009, the branch now has the most intensive service in its history. However, due to tight timing, alternative off-peak trains from Falmouth now omit this stop and other services only stop on request. *David Lawrence/DHM*

PERRANWELL: 'Prairie' tank No 5573 pauses with a Truro to Falmouth service in a pre-nationalisation scene. The train is obscuring the small stone-built main station building. The wooden staircase provides access to the unusual elevated 21-lever signal box, which was erected in 1894 when the siding accommodation here was altered and expanded. The box straddles one siding, with the goods shed out of view to the right. The goods yard closed to general traffic in January 1965 with the three down sidings taken out of use three months later. *Lens of Sutton Association*

Although through coaches had previously operated to Falmouth, a through train from Paddington to Falmouth was introduced on summer weekdays in 1953 to ease the load on the 'Cornish Riviera'. Newquay traffic was also catered for, with three coaches detached at Par. On Saturdays the train ran only to Newquay, though another one ran to Falmouth. All engine types were authorised on this branch, but 'Red' and 'Blue' locos were not to exceed 35mph, and only certain classes were allowed to enter Perranwell and Penryn goods sheds. Viewed from the cattle dock, No 1008 *County of Cardigan* passes Perranwell at 6.04pm on Sunday 6 August 1961. The engine will work tender-first back to Truro, as there was no turntable at Falmouth from about 1925. *R. A. Lumber*

PENRYN: The other original intermediate station was located on a curve, but the station was resited in 1923 when the line was realigned and Penryn Viaduct, just to the north, replaced by an embankment. This photo is of the early stages of this work, with the original station in view, and the site of the new platforms on the left. Part of an up goods train is on the main line with its engine shunting in the goods yard. The original goods shed was retained in the new layout, but with additional sidings provided. The main station building was also kept, and was therefore remote from the new platforms.

The goods yard, crossing loop and signal box were all taken out of use on 7 November 1971. However, in October 2008 work started on a £7.8 million upgrade scheme involving a platform extension, modernised signalling and the installation of a 400-metre passing loop. From 18 May 2009 the previous hourly service was doubled and, as recorded 12 days later, No 153369 has just arrived in Platform 1 via the loop with the 1020 service from Truro. In the distance No 153377 was first to arrive and now awaits departure from Platform 2 as the 1020 service from Falmouth Docks. *Lens of Sutton Association/Nigel Tregoning*

PENMERE: This staffed halt was opened on 1 June 1925 to serve a large housing estate being developed to the south-west of Falmouth. The estimated cost of providing the 300-foot-long platform, booking office, waiting room and access pathway was £854. In 1928 an additional ladies waiting room and lavatories for both ladies and gents were authorised at an estimated cost of £300. The loop on the left of this photo was installed in 1940 and served as a headshunt for an oil depot.

The station has been adopted by the 'Friends of Penmere', a group of local residents, and an attractive brick shelter was erected in 1999. No 150267 calls with the 1237 Truro to Falmouth Docks service on 23 September 2008. Passenger loadings are booming on 'The Maritime Line', with 1997's 156,000 estimated journeys increasing to 261,000 in 2007. *Lens of Sutton Association/DHM*

FALMOUTH is located near the mouth of the wide estuary of Carrick Roads, and the River Fal from which its name is derived actually runs into this estuary about 5 miles to the north. This ancient port has provided shelter to shipping for many hundreds of years and was a Post Office packet port from 1688 to 1852, by which time Southampton had usurped its role, mainly due to having a rail link to London. The railway finally reached Falmouth in 1863 and it was originally planned that the terminus would be sited nearer the town centre, but at that time the Falmouth Docks Co was constructing a new harbour protected by two breakwaters. This development was established as a repair facility with dry docks and deep water wharves. With this traffic potential in mind, it was decided to route the railway around the west side of the town to a location above the new docks. No 4587 waits to leave from the short up platform with a train for Truro, the 'Prairie' being based there from July 1954 until withdrawal in July 1960.

No 150267 is about to leave as the 1459 service to Truro on 23 September 2008. *Lens of Sutton Association/DHM*

FALMOUTH: The original terminus had a 70-foot-span overall roof with separate arrival and departure platforms. The latter was shorter of necessity as the goods yard, with a large wooden shed, was located on this side, and beyond it there was an engine shed and turntable. The latter were removed in 1925, among the many changes made to this site over the years. The arrival platform was also signalled for departures from 1928, this being particularly useful when longer through trains were operated. The overall roof was removed in the early 1950s. In a scene from the departure platform about ten years later, a DMU has arrived on the right, and a Wyman's bookstall can be seen on the left.

The station was closed in 1970 and replaced by a new halt about half a mile away and closer to the town centre, constructed using sections of the platform from Perranporth Beach Halt. However, the original terminus reopened on 5 May 1975, when the 'new' station was re-named 'The Dell'. In 1988 the two stations were named Falmouth Docks and Falmouth Town respectively. Only a shortened arrival platform survives today, with much of the site redeveloped. *Lens of Sutton Association/DHM*

FALMOUTH: The Cornwall Railway extended its broad-gauge track into the docks and provided a network of lines for the docks company that ran on to the wharves and quaysides. The branch leading to the docks diverged from the main branch just before the terminus, and exchange sidings were provided adjacent to the arrival platform. Falmouth Docks Co No 3, built by Hawthorn Leslie in 1926 as its No 3597, is shunting in these sidings on 29 September 1978. A few days later the docks company took delivery of a diesel shunter, and the saddle tank became 'spare'. Surprisingly its boiler was rebuilt in 1984 and the loco saw occasional use until August 1986, when it was probably the last of its kind still active in the UK. Internal docks rail traffic ceased in the 1990s, the connection with the national network having been disused for many years. However, there was a revival at the end of that decade with short-term contracts for EWS bringing household coal in, and shot blast debris out.

Through summer Saturday trains ended in 1969, but these were reinstated in the years from 1976 to 1979. No 50027 arrives with the 0814 train from Truro on 9 July 1977, which will form the 0910 departure to Paddington. *Ian Cavill/Nigel Tregoning*

Chacewater to Penzance

CHACEWATER: Although its old spelling featured in the name of the 1826 Redruth & Chasewater Railway, that mineral line ran from the mining area south of Redruth to the quays at Devoran, and the proposed branch to Chacewater was never finished. Rails finally reached this station, about a mile from its village, when the West Cornwall was extended to Truro Road in 1852. Originally having a single platform, an up one and passing loop were added in 1872. The latter was converted to an island platform in 1912 to cater for Newquay trains, although the branch had actually been operational since 1903. A '45XX' Class 'Prairie' tank waits in this platform with a Newquay train in August 1937.

With the closure of the branch in 1963, the station lost its main raison d'être and was closed on 5 October 1964. The island platform has since been demolished and only an overgrown bank of rubble remains today. Looking back to about 1962, North British Type 2 No D6312 was recorded from the down platform before leaving for Newquay. *R. A. Lumber/Lens of Sutton Association*

DRUMP LANE, REDRUTH: On 17 June 1912 a new goods yard was brought into use by the GWR to replace a small facility adjacent to Redruth station, less than half a mile away. This yard took two years to build and consisted of a long reception loop and a second, parallel loop serving a large goods shed. Another siding served a loading dock and cattle pens, while two others were available for the coal and general merchandise traffic handled by the yard, the heyday of the local mining industry having long passed. The West of England Bacon Curing Co was established here in 1892, and was acquired by C. & T. Harris Ltd of Calne in 1900; a siding served the factory from 1926 to 1966. The factory dominates the background as No D1040 *Western Queen* indulges in some shunting on 19 June 1975.

The factory was demolished in the 1980s, and a housing estate now covers the area. No 150263 forms the 0529 Bristol Temple Meads to Penzance service on 9 October 2008. *Steve Cummins/DHM*

DRUMP LANE, REDRUTH: *Western Queen* is seen again from a footbridge that crosses the site, as it reverses its load towards the 160 feet by 49 feet brick-built goods shed, which had an internal loading platform the length of the building. Just out of view to the left, a partially glazed canopy extended for 135 feet along the south side of the building, affording weather protection over three cart entrances. The goods shed contained two hand cranes with a larger 5-ton crane positioned in the yard. The 29-lever signal box was opened in December 1911 to control all movements relating to the yard.

Drump Lane handled general traffic until May 1967, then continued as an NCL depot until 1979. Most of the trackwork was then soon lifted but the reception loop was retained, primarily to allow locomotives to run round the Chacewater cement trains. However, this practice ceased when the signal box closed on 12 January 1986. The site of the yard is now occupied by a transport and storage company. 'Voyager' No 220032 passes with the 0930 Penzance to Manchester Piccadilly service on 9 October 2008. *Steve Cummins/ DHM*

REDRUTH: Although the Hayle Railway had its eastern terminus in the town, it occupied a different site from that eventually selected by the West Cornwall for its station. The original station was less than half a mile to the west and became a goods depot, reached by a spur from the new main line at a point known as Redruth Junction. The Hayle Railway's 2½-mile-long branch to Tresavean, serving a mining district south-west of Redruth, also left the main line at this location. This branch was taken over by the WCR and remained open until 1936. The present Redruth station is handily placed in the town centre. Viewed from the 1888-vintage footbridge, 'Peak' No 45007 emerges from the short 47-yard-long Redruth Tunnel with the 0805 Bristol Temple Meads to Penzance train on 24 July 1979.

Power car No 43127 leads the arriving 1206 Paddington to Penzance service on 19 September 2008. *Both DHM*

REDRUTH: No 1002 *County of Berks* arrives with a train bound for its Penzance home in June 1958. The brick-built main station building is in view; this replaced the original timber building in the 1930s, and survived damage from an air raid in March 1941. The canopy of the small timber down-side building can be glimpsed above the first coach. At one time there had been a goods yard to the right, but the two sidings were removed following the opening of Drump Lane yard; the platforms were lengthened at the same time. A large Methodist Chapel dominates in the background.

The station is substantially intact today, and Nos 150279/280 leave forming the 1555 Plymouth to Penzance service on 19 September 2008. These Arriva Trains Wales units were on sub-lease to First Great Western at the time. *Norman Simmons/DHM*

REDRUTH: Another 4-6-0, No 6801 *Aylburton Grange*, is coming off the 193-yard-long Redruth Viaduct as it approaches the station with an up train on the same day. This engine was allocated to Penzance throughout the 1950s. From 1914 to 1955 there had been a 34-lever signal box at the west end of the down platform (just to the left of this view). After its closure, the up siding in the foreground was worked by a ground frame supervised from Drump Lane signal box. A spur runs past the camera to a goods loading dock on the site of a former timber-built goods shed. Carn Brea Hill can be seen in the right background, once home to an Iron Age hill camp; today it is crowned by a ruined castle, and a monument erected in 1836 to commemorate Francis Basset, a wealthy industrialist.

The siding was removed in 1964, and today's undergrowth dictated a slightly different position to view an HST set departing for Penzance. *Norman Simmons/DHM*

CARN BREA: This West Cornwall Railway station was located close to the site of the Hayle Railway's Pool station. Opening on 25 August 1852, five months after the line, it was itself renamed Pool from 1854 to 1875. This undated photo from the station's later days is looking west from the down platform towards Camborne, and includes the main station building. Behind the camera are two goods yards on the up side, one adjacent to the station, with the other about a quarter of a mile further east at the site of the original WCR locomotive works and also at the junction with a mineral branch that ran for a little over 3 miles to the small port of Portreath on the north coast. This line was opened by the HR in 1837 and closed in sections from 1936 to 1938. More than half a mile to the west of Carn Brea, another short HR branch ran to North Crofty, serving tin and copper mines; the final portion closed in 1948.

This station was the most lightly used between Truro and Penzance and was an early casualty, closing on 2 January 1961. The two yards were taken out of use in 1965-67. A modern public footbridge crosses the site of the station and in two 9 October 2008 views we see first power car No 43161 leading the 1000 Penzance to Paddington service. Turning the other way, No 150219 passes the site of the platforms with the 0646 Bristol to Penzance service. *Lens of Sutton Association/DHM (2)*

ROSKEAR JUNCTION: Another branch of the HR was opened on 23 December 1837 through the eastern suburbs of Camborne to serve several tin and copper mines, primarily delivering coal to feed the boilers and pumping engines. The line ran for only just under a mile to the terminus at North Roskear and had no fewer than six level crossings. In 1839 the Holman Bros mining machinery works was established in Camborne, and the branch also served the company's boiler works and foundry. Holman's became world-renowned for its rock drills. The branch was originally worked from a ground frame, but a 29-lever signal box was provided near the junction in 1895. The junction layout changed in March 1975 when the crossover to the down main was removed, with all access then being only from the up main line. Adjacent to the signal box are a level crossing and footbridge, and No 25223 is seen from the latter while leaving the branch on 21 June 1978.

The signal box survives as a block post but the frame was removed in the early 1990s; it now controls two local manual crossings, and supervises two other crossings at Dolcoath and Gwinear Road. No 150234 approaches forming the 1244 Plymouth to Penzance service on 25 September 2008. *Ian Cavill/DHM*

ROSKEAR BRANCH: No working of the branch was allowed after dark, but that portion from the catch point near the junction for about 350 yards to the gates of the first level crossing (Foundry Lane) could be used for refuging main-line freights when the branch was not occupied by another train. A short siding with a wagon weighbridge of 60-ton capacity was added about 150 yards from the junction in 1943. The line beyond Holman's No 3 Foundry was officially closed in 1963, though traffic beyond there had probably ceased many years before. Then in 1966 a loop and loading platform were added between the weighbridge siding and Foundry Lane. The line north of this crossing was sold to Holmans in 1970. Traffic was sporadic in later years and photos of trains on this branch are rare, but No 25223 was recorded looking south from Foundry Lane on 21 June 1978; the loop siding is on the left.

Latter-day traffic included the despatch of compressor plant, but this petered out and the branch was closed in January 1981. In recent years the alignment of Foundry Lane has been changed and the 'present' view from a supermarket car park belies any suggestion of a railway ever having been here. However, the housing to the right of the loco can still be seen in 2008. *Ian Cavill/DHM*

CAMBORNE could be considered to have been the 'capital' of West Cornwall's mining industry, and is the home of the world-famous Camborne School of Mines. For many years a daily pick-up goods would leave Truro at 4.48am to serve various sidings en route to here, and 0-6-0PT No 3702 and brake-van are seen from the station's plate girder footbridge as they commence the return journey on 15 July 1961. The engine will work the Roskear branch if required and further calls will be made at Carn Brea yard and Drump Lane on its way home.

The town's current population is estimated at 22,500. However, it abuts the neighbouring settlements of Redruth and Pool, thus forming the largest urban conurbation in Cornwall, and the combined population is almost twice this figure. No 150127 calls with the 1255 Penzance to Plymouth service on 25 September 2008.
Peter W. Gray/DHM

CAMBORNE station is seen from the up platform, probably in the 1950s, with the main brick-built structure containing the booking office, waiting rooms and toilets on the left. Flanking it on the nearside is a wooden hut, while the 35-lever signal box can be glimpsed on its far side adjacent to a level crossing. The box opened in 1895 when the line was doubled to Roskear Junction. There is also a substantial waiting room on the down platform, which was shorter than the up one (particularly so after the latter had been lengthened in 1937), due to the presence of sidings that form part of the goods yard. Just visible in the foreground is a crossover that provides access from the yard to the up main line.

The signal box closed in June 1970 when automatic barriers were installed at the crossing, controlled from Roskear Junction box. The goods yard closed in 1964 with all the track taken out of use the following year; this eventually allowed the down platform to be extended in 1980. The substantial goods shed still stands and is used by a builders' merchant. The September 2008 scene shows that most of the platform structures have been removed, with basic shelters provided. However, the main building survives, minus its awning, and contains a privately owned buffet; the booking office is open during part of the day. *Lens of Sutton Association/DHM*

CAMBORNE From just to the east of Roskear Junction the line westward descends for 2 miles at a ruling gradient of 1 in 55. Camborne station can be glimpsed in the background as No 6870 *Bodicote Grange* makes a spirited departure down the grade with a train for Penzance on 15 July 1961. Although the 'Hall' Class were fine performers over the undulating Cornish main line, with their smaller driving wheels (5ft 8in as opposed to 6 feet), and slightly higher tractive effort, the 'Granges' were considered to be the ideal engine on this route, particularly for their hill-climbing attributes. The class could be found on all manner of duties and Penzance regularly had an allocation of ten or so through the 1950s; indeed, just prior to the start of dieselisation about 30% of the 80-strong class were allocated to Plymouth Laira and the three main Cornish sheds.

On 25 September 2008 Nos 43079 and 43125 power the 0730 Paddington to Penzance service through the heavily overgrown cutting. *Peter W. Gray/DHM*

GWINEAR ROAD: Although the amount of goods traffic originating here was modest, extensive siding accommodation was provided for marshalling trains and wagon storage, particularly in connection with the area's vibrant agricultural traffic. The sizeable east yard was in use by the early years of the 20th century, with additional sidings provided in 1915. Photographed from the cattle dock, 4-6-0 No 6863 *Dolhywel Grange* runs around the sharp curve on the approach to the station with a down goods on 9 April 1960. The up loop is on the extreme left, with the down refuge siding to the right of the train. Beyond this, 2-6-2Ts Nos 4564 and 5546 are in the yard, at the far end of which stands the 15-lever East box. This came into use in 1900 when the line from Camborne was doubled. In the foreground the cattle dock siding joins the branch to Helston.

Apart from the main running lines, all this track was taken out of use in the period between 1962 and 1965, culminating in the closure of East box. A short section of track can, however, be seen next to the cattle dock as No 150127 sweeps by forming the 1038 Plymouth to Penzance service on 9 October 2008. *P. Q. Treloar/DHM*

GWINEAR ROAD station had a single platform on the down side in HR and WCR days, but was rebuilt for the opening of the Helston branch in 1887, when two platforms were provided, branch services using the outer face of the down island platform. St Blazey's No 5926 *Grotrian Hall* passes over the level crossing immediately to the east of the station with an up train in 1953. The 49-lever West signal box is just visible on the left. This replaced its predecessor on the opposite side of the line in 1916, a year after the line west to Angarrack was doubled.

With no population centre close by, the closure of the Helston branch in 1962 deprived Gwinear Road of most of its passenger traffic and the station closed from 5 October 1964. West box closed on 31 October 1965 when automatic half-barriers were brought into use. Evidence of the down platform can be noted as No 150219 approaches forming the 1142 Penzance to Plymouth service on 9 October 2008. *P. Q. Treloar/DHM*

GWINEAR ROAD: 'Mogul' No 6319 runs under the station footbridge with a down parcels train at 4.10pm on 24 July 1957; the leading vehicle is an empty six-wheel milk tank, probably bound for St Erth. 'Prairie' tank No 4505 waits in the branch platform with the 4.12pm to Helston. The parcels working could be a late-running 10.40pm from Paddington, which was due here at 2.45pm; its run to Penzance was scheduled to take no less than 16¾ hours in all! However, there would have been much shunting en route with traffic detached at various locations, and other vehicles added, particularly at Bristol, where vans from Manchester and Birmingham would join the consist. *Peter W. Gray*

Viewed from the footbridge, No 6826 *Nannerth Grange* and a '43XX' Class 'Mogul' double-head an express from Penzance to the North, probably on a summer Saturday in 1959. A good view is gained of the station buildings; that on the up side has a single-pitch roof that continued over the platform as a canopy. At some stage this roof was extended at the east end to cover more of the platform. The platforms were lengthened when the line west was doubled, and beyond these there were two sidings on the up side. *P. Q. Treloar*

ST ERTH: Apart from a deviation to avoid a rope-worked incline west of Camborne, the West Cornwall followed the route of the earlier Hayle Railway from Redruth until about three-quarters of a mile west of Gwinear Road. From here a new alignment, avoiding another incline at Angarrack, was used to reach Hayle. Only about 1½ miles further on from Hayle on the new route to Penzance, St Ives Road station was provided, its name referring to the fishing village and developing resort some 3 miles to the north-west. The station was rebuilt and renamed for the opening of the St Ives branch in 1877. No 6845 *Paviland Grange* has just picked up additional traffic from the goods sidings on the right and is waiting to leave with the 1.35pm broccoli special from Ponsandane yard on 6 April 1960.

Today the station shows little evidence of 'modernisation' and retains much of its character. No 150279 leaves as the 1255 Penzance to Plymouth service on 19 September 2008. *P. Q. Treloar/DHM*

95

ST ERTH: As rebuilt in 1875-76, the station comprised a single platform for main-line trains with a bay for branch services. A down loop and platform were added about 20 years later, and both main-line platforms were extended westwards in 1904. Two refuge sidings were provided at the east end of the station on the down side, each of which at the height of the summer season could be used for stabling 10-coach trains. No 7916 *Mobberley Hall* enters the up platform at 1.35pm on 14 July 1962 with the 1.20pm 'all stations' stopper from Penzance to Truro. The rear of the 11.50pm Liverpool to Penzance, hauled by 'Warship' No D861 *Vigilant*, can be glimpsed in the distance. On leaving St Erth the 'Hall' will descend at 1 in 70 for a short distance, but will then be climbing for more than 4 miles to Gwinear Road.

The station's 1899-vintage signal box is still open, though only about a half of its 69-lever frame is used today. The surviving semaphores add to the pleasing ambience, as do the palm trees on both platforms. Power cars Nos 43087 and 43186 arrive with the 1400 Penzance to Paddington service on 19 September 2008. *Peter W. Gray/DHM*

ST ERTH: Penzance-based 4-6-0 No 4095 *Harlech Castle* attacks the 1 in 67 grade as it pulls out of St Erth with a down express on 26 July 1958. 'Castle' Class engines started to appear on the Cornish main line prior to the Second World War, and in BR days the type regularly appeared on the 'Cornish Riviera Express', Penzance having an allocation of one or two examples through the 1950s – the only Cornish shed to do so. During this time, however, the majority of main-line passenger workings were handled by 'Counties', 'Halls' and 'Granges', with no clear pattern as to what type would appear on a specific train. In the early 1950s BR Standard 'Britannia' Class 'Pacifics' were introduced on the 'Cornish Riviera', but this type proved unpopular with the local enginemen. *P. Q. Treloar*

MARAZION: When passing through Hayle, the line is close to the north coast, but within 4 miles of leaving St Erth the rails have crossed Cornwall's narrowest point, and reach the shores of Mount's Bay on the south coast. Here passengers have a fine view of St Michael's Mount, rising 230 feet above the sea and crowned with a castle. The line was doubled between St Erth and Marazion in June 1929, and a bridge carrying the road from Penzance to the village of Marazion was erected to replace a level crossing at the east end of the station. In a view therefrom, No 6860 *Aberporth Grange* approaches with broccoli empties on 6 April 1960. Two pairs of sidings were provided on each side of the line at about the time of the doubling, and were used for both carriage and wagon storage; on this occasion those on the up side contain the inevitable cattle wagons for perishable traffic.

The sidings were removed by 1966 when the signal box closed. No 150249 forms the 1244 Plymouth to Penzance service on 26 September 2008. *P. Q. Treloar/DHM*

MARAZION: When opened by the WCR in 1852, the station had a single platform with a timber building and was named Marazion Road; the village was half a mile to the east. Built in a low-lying marshy area, the train service was frequently disrupted by the weather in early years. The station was rebuilt prior to the line being doubled to Ponsandane in 1893, and renamed three years after this. Extensive goods facilities were provided here with the main goods yard on the up side, where a large loading wharf was provided for the perishable traffic, much of which was despatched to London. The main station building was on the down side with a smaller waiting room on the opposite platform, both built of granite blocks. A signal box was located further west on the down platform and a camping coach was provided here from 1937. 'Castle' Class No 5062 *Earl of Shaftesbury* waits with an up parcels train on Monday 9 June 1958.

Passenger traffic ceased from 5 October 1964 but the main building survives and is passed by No 43024 heading the 1400 Penzance to Paddington HST on 26 September 2008. *P. K. Tunks/DHM*

99

PENZANCE SHED: There had been at least two earlier depots close to Penzance station before a new shed was opened in 1914 at a site officially known as Ponsandane, more than a mile to the east of the terminus. Over the years the location became known as Long Rock, its local name. A standard four-road straight building, large enough for 12 tender locos, was erected in brick, with a single-road repair shop on the north side. Coded 83G in BR days, two of its resident 4-6-0s Nos 4908 *Broome Hall* and 1018 *County of Leicester* stand over the inspection pits outside the running shed on Wednesday 11 June 1958. The turntable is just to the left of this view. Access to the shed was controlled from Long Rock signal box, which stood next to the down main less than half a mile west of Marazion station.

In 1959 a screen was erected down the centre of the shed to segregate the new diesels from steam locos. Most of the depot's main-line steam engines were transferred away by the middle of 1960, with Laira-based diesel-hydraulics handling much of the long-distance traffic. It finally closed to steam in September 1962. The depot was recoded to 84D in 1963 when Laira became a District shed. Three Class 42 'Warships' are resting outside the depot on 13 January 1970; from left to right, they are Nos 821 *Greyhound*, 803 *Albion* and 829 *Magpie*.

The shed was eventually demolished to make way for a new HST depot, with work commencing in March 1976. The 'new' shed is a single-track structure, 750 feet long with a maintenance pit throughout its length. The depot is at its busiest overnight when engaged in servicing a number of HST and 'Voyager' sets. When this photo was taken on 26 September 2008, the only passenger stock on site was the sleeper train, which was inside the shed. A train of fuel tanks is on the right; the weekly delivery of gas oil is currently the only regular freight traffic west of Burngullow. The main line is in the foreground; single-line working was introduced west of Marazion in 1974. *P. K. Tunks/John Medley/DHM*

In another scene from 11 June 1958, Truro's No 6911 *Holker Hall* is next to the coal stage; the main line is further to the left. At this time the shed had an allocation of 33 engines; in addition to the two previously pictured locos, these were 'Castle' 4-6-0 No 4095, 'County' 4-6-0 Nos 1002/06/08, 'Modified Hall' 4-6-0 No 7925, 'Hall' 4-6-0s Nos 4931/50 and 5934/72, 'Grange' 4-6-0 Nos 6800/01/08/16/24/25/26/37/60/70/75, 2-6-2Ts Nos 4545/47/54/63/66/70/77, and 0-6-0PTs Nos 8409/73, 9463 and 9748. *P. K. Tunks*

PENZANCE SHED: The 65-foot-diameter turntable was used by a steam engine for the last time on 3 May 1964, after Bulleid 'Pacific' No 34002 *Salisbury* arrived with 'The Cornubian', a PRC/RCTS special from Exeter to Penzance that was to be the final steam-hauled train over the Cornish main line until the GW150 celebrations in 1985. The shed's sand-drying furnace is beyond the DMU to the left, with the coal stage on the right, complete with its 45,000-gallon water tank. If the Penzance turntable was out of action, the nearest means of turning locos was at Truro, more than 24 miles away. An indication of the difficulties that this could cause arose in 1956, when this turntable was under repair from 22 May to 15 June. Eighteen large 'Prairie' tanks were sent to Truro and Penzance from other WR depots on loan, and these worked many of the main-line trains between the two places, with most of the home tender engines sent away in exchange. The turntable was removed in 1966. *R. A. Lumber*

PONSANDANE YARD: With facilities at the terminus somewhat cramped, developments to the east commenced in about 1871 with the construction of a goods siding, together with a loading platform, primarily for horticultural traffic. Over the years improvements were made, particularly in the 1930s when further goods and carriage sidings were provided. Additional goods platforms allowed four trains to be handled simultaneously, and a large goods shed was opened in 1937. No D1006 *Western Stalwart* is next to one of the loading docks as it awaits departure with what is probably 6B59, the 1450 Ponsandane to Exeter Riverside freight, on 7 February 1972. Beyond the rear of the train is an occupation crossing to the beach, and next to this, though barely visible, is the 39-lever flat-roofed Ponsandane signal box.

The box was in use from 1912 to 1974 and the goods shed closed in 1978. A footbridge has replaced the crossing, and this can be noted in the background as No 150232 passes the disused goods platforms on 26 September 2008 with the 1255 Penzance to Plymouth service. *John Medley/DHM*

PENZANCE: The four-platform terminus, complete with its overall roof, can be seen in the distance as station pilot No 8473 shunts empty stock at about 2.50pm on Whit Monday, 6 June 1960. This engine had been allocated new to Penzance in September 1951, when it joined sister No 8409. The latter was also new when it arrived in early 1950 to take over the pilot duties hitherto performed by pannier tank No 2097 of 1897 vintage. The signal box with its 75-lever frame opened on 24 April 1938, replacing an earlier structure sited a little further to the west. The 'new' box was located approximately on the site of the original engine shed.

Although there have been changes to the trackwork, the view today is little changed. The signal box is still open and controls the line as far as Marazion; its semaphores were replaced by colour light signals in December 1981. Two single units, Nos 153373 and 153361, depart for Exeter St David's at 1644 on 22 September 2008. *Derek Frost/DHM*

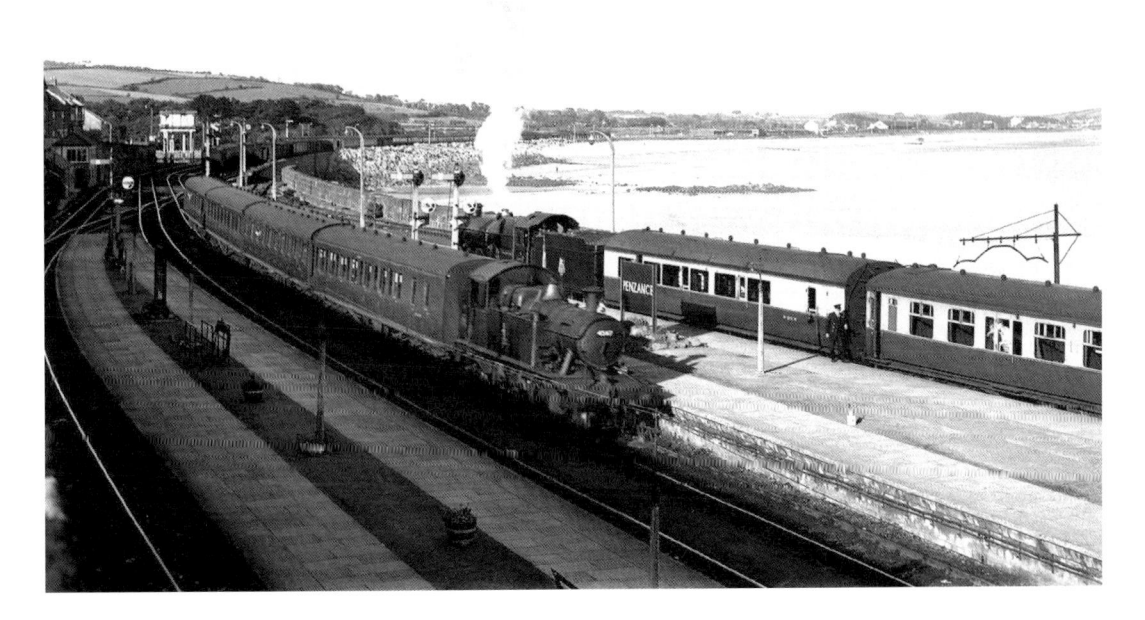

PENZANCE: 'Prairie' tank No 4547 arrives in Platform No 3 at 6.18pm on Wednesday 21 August 1957 with the 5.18pm from Truro, while 'Castle' Class No 5091 *Cleeve Abbey* awaits its 6.30pm departure from No 4 with a return excursion to Paignton and Exeter. The railway skirts Mount's Bay for about 2 miles from Penzance, and Ponsandane goods shed and Long Rock depot can be glimpsed above the second coach of the excursion. Out of the picture to the right, the station has three additional bays for parcels and sundries traffic, and Bristol Bath Road's No 6951 *Impney Hall* is standing at one of these with the 6.40pm Travelling Post Office to Paddington.

Mail traffic ended in early 2004, but excursion traffic, some steam-hauled, still uses these platforms on occasions. More typical, though, is another pair of single units, Nos 153377 and 153305, which are seen arriving with the 1401 service from Plymouth on 26 September 2008. *R. A. Lumber/DHM*

PENZANCE: Viewed from the end of Platform 2, 'Castle' 4-6-0 No 5075 *Wellington* backs into Platform 4 from where it will head another return excursion in May 1959. A '94XX' Class station pilot and shunters' truck are visible in the background; Penzance had received its first diesel shunter (D3514) the previous August, and this type would soon take over such duties. *R. A. Lumber*

The legendary *City of Truro* has already been seen in these pages during its current period of use, but this photo dates from Whit Sunday, 25 May 1958, when the 1903-built 4-4-0 worked the 9.35am from Exeter St David's to Penzance, a BR-sponsored amateur photographers' excursion. Prizes were offered for the best photographs taken during the trip by the occupants of the well-filled six-coach train, which is seen just before commencing its return journey. No 3440 had emerged from a 26-year-long sojourn in the old York Railway Museum in 1957, and on 15 September that year worked an excursion from Plymouth to Penzance. Ten minutes was allowed at Truro for watering, and it is likely that this was its very first visit to its namesake city, as it is doubtful whether any of the 'Cities' were seen west of Plymouth during their working lives. *R. A. Lumber*

PENZANCE: The West Cornwall's line into its terminus was carried over the beach on an extremely exposed 347-yard-long timber viaduct. Although providing pleasing views to the traveller, the structure was damaged by gales on a number of occasions before being demolished completely in a dreadful storm in 1869. Initially the line was temporarily moved inland, but a new viaduct, 3 feet higher and with granite piers at the western end, was opened in 1871. This was still susceptible to the elements, however, and the line was only really protected when the viaduct was replaced by a substantial stone embankment in 1921. This ran for a quarter of a mile along the shoreline and carried both the newly double-tracked main line and siding accommodation. No 6805 *Broughton Grange* has arrived in Platform 2 on 6 June 1960.

Today Paddington trains normally use Platform 1, and the 1600 departure is leaving on 22 September 2008. *Derek Frost/DHM*

PENZANCE: The original terminus was very cramped, but was reconstructed by the GWR in 1879 when the present train shed was erected, though only two short platforms were provided at that time. Today's station basically dates from 1937 when it was rebuilt and enlarged using land reclaimed from the sea. Four platform faces were provided, each able to handle a 12-coach train, with three of these protected by the overall roof at their westernmost ends. Platforms 3 and 4 were slightly shorter to allow access to the loading bays in the yard. The main stone-built station buildings were situated at right angles to and behind the buffer stops. Due to the lie of the land, the booking office was at a higher level and access to the platforms was via stairways and a raised balcony. No 6836 *Estevarney Grange* has arrived at mainland Britain's most westerly terminus with the 12.25am train from Manchester on 6 June 1960, with No 6805 *Broughton Grange* seen again on the left.

On 26 September 2008 Nos 153305 and 153377 depart as the 1644 service to Exeter. *Derek Frost/DHM*

Helston branch

PRAZE: This line was built to standard gauge by local promoters, the Helston Railway Company. However, the Great Western worked the branch from its opening on 9 May 1887, and took over the company completely in 1898. From the junction at Gwinear Road the line headed south for just over 2¾ miles before reaching the first of the two original intermediate stations, which was sited close to the village of Praze-an-Beeble. The station had a single platform, and a goods loop served the yard, which was worked from a ground frame. The points at the south end were removed in about 1950, leaving a siding facing towards Gwinear Road. 'Prairie' tank No 4570 passes the sizeable water tank as it arrives with the 2.25pm Gwinear Road to Helston train on 11 July 1961; the ground frame was contained in the hut at the far end of the substantial stone building.

After closure the site was cleared and a dwelling was erected here in about 1991; all evidence of the station has vanished. *Peter W. Gray/DHM*

NANCEGOLLAN: The other original intermediate station was situated about 5 miles from Gwinear Road and had a single platform with a goods loop and single siding. A passing loop with signal box was installed about half a mile to the north of the station in 1908. This was taken out of use in 1937 when the station was reconstructed with two platforms. A sizeable goods yard was also provided, the layout controlled from a 30-lever signal box. The station was surrounded by good agricultural land and acted as a railhead for a widespread rural area; in particular it dealt with large quantities of new potatoes, broccoli and early spring flowers. No 4552 is busy shunting the yard while working the 2.05pm goods from Helston on 14 April 1960. This view is from an overbridge that has a steel span over the track leading to the 'new' sidings, and a stone arch over the running lines (out of view to the left).

The bridge survives today but the site of the yard has been redeveloped. *P. Q. Treloar/DHM*

TRUTHALL HALT opened on 1 July 1905 in a somewhat isolated spot adjacent to a minor road. It was officially designated in the timetable as 'Platform' from July 1906, reverting to its original title at a later date. However, tickets referred to 'Truthall Bridge Halt'! Originally constructed of timber with a galvanised 'Pagoda' shelter, at some stage the platform was rebuilt and reduced in length. The 'new' platform could accommodate a single coach and is pictured in its latter days.

After the branch closed, part of the trackbed was acquired by the Trevarno Estate, whose gardens are open to the public. Much of the formation became heavily overgrown, but a fledgling preservation group is working towards reopening a section of the branch. Based at Trevarno, around a quarter of a mile of track has been laid northwards from there, with another quarter-mile of the formation south cleared to the site of this halt. Viewed from the bridge, the remains of the platform are on the right. *Lens of Sutton Collection/DHM*

TRUTHALL HALT: Looking south from the same bridge on 15 July 1961, 2-6-2T No 4588 is accelerating away with the 2.25pm from Gwinear Road, after stopping to pick up two passengers at the halt. In less than a mile the train will cross Cober Viaduct, the most substantial engineering feature on the branch. Built of granite from a nearby quarry, this 121-yard-long structure is 90 feet high and has six arches.

This part of the trackbed is still heavily overgrown and the other obvious difference from the 'past' picture is the extent to which Helston has expanded on the distant hillside. *Peter W. Gray/DHM*

Cober Viaduct is pictured rising from the vegetation. There are long-term plans for the revived railway to cross this, and terminate at a new station located in an industrial estate on the outskirts of Helston. *DHM*

HELSTON: The branch was classified as an 'Uncoloured' route, but as a concession to some stiff gradients '45XX' tanks were permitted to work the line. Other types such as '43XX' Class 'Moguls' and '51XX' 2-6-2Ts were also allowed between Gwinear Road and Nancegollan. No 4553 is seen from an overbridge while in the terminus on Friday 13 June 1958. The single-road stone-built engine shed is just in view on the right; this sub-shed of Penzance would house a single '45XX' overnight. When goods traffic was particularly heavy three of the class could be found on the branch each day, with two engaged in working mixed and goods trains. The former iron ore wagons on the left are standing on a recently laid siding that is on the same site as one taken up many years previously. It was reinstated for the loading of serpentine, a local stone found on The Lizard.

Much of the site is now covered by housing, and rather than include a photo of this, a second view from the same day shows No 4553 waiting at the platform with the 3.20pm departure for Gwinear Road. *Both P. K. Tunks*

HELSTON: Britain's most southerly terminus was built as a through station, with the expectation in the branch's early years that it would be extended into the Lizard peninsula. However, the GWR introduced a pioneering omnibus service from Helston to The Lizard in 1903 and any such thoughts were soon forgotten. The substantial goods shed can be noted in the background as No 4566 is engaged in shunting activity on 13 April 1956.

This was the last wholly steam-worked WR line in Cornwall and when diesels finally arrived in 1962 it was in form of North British Type 2s rather than DMUs, due to the still considerable freight traffic. Although passenger numbers were boosted by traffic from the Royal Naval Air Station at nearby Culdrose, local usage was low and the branch closed to this traffic from 5 November 1962. Goods services continued until total closure on 4 October 1964. The goods shed still survives, and has been incorporated in a housing development for the elderly; a short section of the platform can also be noted on the right. All the 'present' images on this branch were taken on 9 October 2008. *Terry Gough/DHM*

Hayle wharves branch

HAYLE: The Hayle Railway served this mining port, running from a terminus at Hayle Foundry on the quayside, before crossing Copperhouse Creek by way of a drawbridge, then heading eastwards along the north side of the creek. This section was bypassed when the railway was absorbed and rebuilt by the West Cornwall; the latter's line entered the town on a higher alignment, with a station sited adjacent to a viaduct that carried the new route westwards over both the port area and the site of the HR's terminus. However, the WCR provided access to the wharves via a new heavily graded branch, which diverged from the main line on the up side, between this viaduct and the station. Pannier tank No 3635 propels its train down the 1 in 30 incline from the station to the wharves at 11.25am on 14 July 1961.

After closure the trackbed was used as a footpath that provided access to the station, but in 2006 Network Rail fenced this off due to misuse of the station foot crossing. The formation is now heavily overgrown – only the occupation bridge (just) links these views. *Peter W. Gray/DHM*

HAYLE: 'Prairie' tank No 4571 is crossing the main A30 road on 4 July 1959 after picking up wagons from Penpol Sidings; the rest of its train is on the right, beyond the swing bridge over the entrance to Copperhouse Creek. The roof of the Wharf signal box can be seen above the engine. Instructions for working were as follows: 'The Train Staff must be shown to the Signalman at Hayle, or the Porter Signalman at Hayle Wharves, as the case may be, before the commencement of each trip. The line falls 1 in 30 for a distance of 300 yards from the station. Before entering upon the falling gradient a Porter must apply sufficient wagon brakes, and the Guard must be in the van and keep his van brake in reserve for emergency. When the rails are slippery the Station Master must arrange to have sand placed upon them between the Wharf Signal box and the Catch points, which are situated nine yards from the Hayle Wharf Home Signal, a distance of 160 yards. When trains are drawn from the station to the wharf, the Incline Instructions must be strictly adhered to. When trains are propelled, the Driver must give two short sharp whistles when sufficient brakes are put down to indicate to the Guard that the brake power is sufficient to control the train. Trains must not be propelled from the Wharf to the station.'

The signal box was closed in 1964 when the crossing gates were replaced by lifting barriers, and the A30 now bypasses the town. The swing bridge survives and is used to gain access to the north side of the harbour. *P. Q. Treloar/DHM*

HAYLE: A line from Penpol Sidings ran along Penpol Terrace on the original alignment of the Hayle Railway, and beneath the main line. At one time this served a gasworks and Harvey's Iron Foundry on the west wharf. The foundry closed in 1904 but the line continued to serve the company's activities as merchants. Locomotives were banned from this section and trains were worked by horses, as illustrated in another scene from 4 July 1959 where a 'double-header' pauses while working two box vans towards the town. No 4571 can be glimpsed crossing the 277-yard-long Hayle Viaduct after leaving the wharves branch. Equine operation is normally associated with early tramways, and it is perhaps surprising that some 9,000 horses were acquired by the British Transport Commission at nationalisation in 1948, many being employed in shunting goods yards.

Horse operations ended here in April 1961, after which a tractor was used for a short period before this section was closed. Penpol Sidings were taken out of use in 1966. *P. Q. Treloar/DHM*

HAYLE: The branch over the swing bridge led to a large number of sidings serving coal wharves and a power station among others. Trailing off to the north-east, another branch followed the route of the old Hayle Railway main line for 1½ miles to access sand pits. During the First World War a short-lived line was laid from this branch to an explosives factory. A siding was installed adjacent to the power station in 1942 for the British Ethyl Corporation, and following a number of corporate changes this was used by Esso to serve an oil distribution depot. This was the last rail traffic to run to the wharves, and No 25057 is waiting to leave with empty tanks on 26 July 1979. The power station closed about this time – its chimneys can be seen in the background.

This final part of the wharves rail system closed in January 1981, and the power station was demolished later that year. All the 'present' photos of the wharves network date from 19 September 2008, when short sections of track could still be found embedded in the ground. *Both DHM*

St Ives branch

ST ERTH: The bay platform provided for the branch's opening on 1 June 1877 is at a lower level than the adjacent up main platform, and a canopy is angled in such a way as to provide protection for both levels (as seen on page 95). No 4540 is running round beyond this canopy at 1.40pm on Wednesday 24 July 1957 after arriving from St Ives. The goods yard is on the left. A loop siding for china clay traffic was laid on its north side in 1927, but was little used and within a few years was instead serving the creamery that can be seen in the background. Large volumes of milk were despatched every day from here to London.

Goods facilities were withdrawn in 1967 and the milk traffic ended in 1980. Now only a siding next to the branch platform survives for engineering use, though scrap metal traffic was loaded here for a short time in about 1999. No 150265 leaves forming the 1411 service to St Ives on 19 September 2008; the signal box can be glimpsed beyond the bracket signal on the right. *Peter W. Gray/DHM*

LELANT SALTINGS: 'Prairie' tank No 4570 is just about to pass under the A30 as it approaches St Erth at 1.12pm on Sunday 6 August 1961. In the background the branch curves away to the right alongside the estuary of the River Hayle.

The road bridge survives, but is now disused, having been replaced by two bridges on either side of it, which form part of a roundabout. No 150267 approaches as the 1525 departure from St Ives on 22 September 2008. Lelant Saltings station can be noted to the left of the post on the right of the picture. This 'park-and-ride' facility opened on 27 May 1978 in an attempt to cure chronic road traffic congestion in St Ives. A car park for 300 vehicles was built beside the new platform, but such was the station's success that both the car park and platform were soon extended. *R. A. Lumber/DHM*

LELANT was one of the original stations, just over a mile from the junction, and was located close to its village. Rather unusually a wooden building was provided, but this was erected on a deep concrete base due to its proximity to the shoreline. This was the last broad-gauge branch to be built, but mixed-gauge operation was introduced from St Erth and on to a spur that left the branch a short distance beyond the station. This led to a quay that had been built out into the estuary, and a small signal box was provided at the station to work this line when it opened in October 1888. The spur closed in about 1914, but its route can be noted just to the left of No 4570 as it leaves Lelant with the 4.12pm from St Erth on 4 August 1961.

The station is now a request stop, with only a limited number of trains scheduled to call. The building is occupied privately, with cream teas available in the summer. The embankment from which the 'past' photo was taken is now heavily overgrown so the view of No 150247 is from an occupation bridge, a little further to the north. The 1506 from St Erth was photographed on 28 September 2008. *Peter W. Gray/DHM*

BETWEEN LELANT AND CARBIS BAY Nos 4554 and 4568 slog up the 1 in 60 gradient above the dunes behind Porth Kidney Sands with the down 'Cornish Riviera' on 30 August 1958. The entrance to Hayle estuary and harbour is above the train, with Hayle's power station in the right background. Two through trains from Paddington operated to St Ives on summer Saturdays, one being a 'dated' overnight working that detached a three-coach portion for the branch at St Erth. However, the first ten coaches of the famed 10.30am departure (the maximum that could be handled at the terminus) worked through to St Ives, with four vehicles for Penzance having been detached at Truro. The branch had no passing loops and was worked as one long block section; the 'express' therefore had to also provide a local service.

Steam returned to the branch after 45 years when LMS 5MT 4-6-0 No 45407 headed the 'St Ives Steamer', the 1437 from Penzance, on a dull and blustery 25 March 2007. *Peter W. Gray/DHM*

122

NEAR CARBIS BAY: A little further on the line curves on a ledge above the end of the beach and reaches its summit, almost 150 feet above sea level, as it enters a 57-foot-deep cutting though a headland called Carrack Gladden. This postcard view taken from a footbridge in the early 1950s includes a 'Prairie' tank approaching this cutting with a train from St Ives. The arc of Carbis Bay's sandy beach lies below, helping to show that the branch offers some of the most spectacular coastal scenery to be seen through a carriage window anywhere. Since their introduction in 1906, '44XX' Class 2-6-2Ts had dominated operations on this branch, but these were superseded by the larger-wheeled '45XX' Class from 1931. This type remained in command until the end of steam working, though only the lighter original engines in the 4500-74 number series were permitted on this line.

On 19 March 1994 Nos 50050 *Fearless* and 50007 *Sir Edward Elgar* (with 50033 *Glorious* at the far end) return from St Ives with the 'Cornish Caper' charter. *Author's collection/DHM*

CARBIS BAY: The railway helped the development of what had been a small community, and the town is now a popular holiday resort, with many hotels and guesthouses catering for visitors attracted to its golden sands and views of the Atlantic Ocean. The station was built on the hillside high above the beach and was originally provided with a 300-foot-long platform; this was extended to 430 feet in 1900. A waiting room was sited on the platform, but the booking office was at a higher level on the station approach road. No 4571 waits to leave with the 4.20pm service from St Ives on 30 July 1960; the footpath on the left leads up to the booking office.

The station building and waiting room have been demolished, with only a small shelter provided today. No 150267 leaves as the 1256 service from St Ives on 22 September 2008. *Peter W. Gray/DHM*

CARBIS BAY: A little beyond the station the line crosses the lofty four-arch 78-yard-long Carbis Bay Viaduct and continues towards Porthminster Point on a ledge on the hillside that affords further spectacular views of the coastline. No 4566 passes the St Ives fixed Distant signal with the 1.30pm train from St Erth on 9 September 1961. On fine days this area of Cornwall has a quality of light that gives the landscape a remarkable definition and clarity, with an intensity of colour that is not to be found elsewhere in Britain. By the early years of the 20th century there was a flourishing colony of artists in St Ives and by the 1930s it was an art centre with an international reputation. The visual arts are now a major factor in the county's economy, and the Tate St Ives gallery, opened in 1993, houses a collection of works by notable local artists.
Peter W. Gray

ST IVES: A Home signal was sited in the cutting at Porthminster Point, and this was kept at 'danger' so that down trains were brought to a stand before being admitted to the station. This was due to a ruling gradient of 1 in 60 and a sharp curve on the final approach to the terminus. A short spur that gave access to the stone-built single-road engine shed trailed in from the left just before the branch crossed Porthminster Viaduct and entered the station. On 4 August 1961 No 4570 arrives in the curving platform with the 1.30pm from St Erth. To save running-round time during the intense summer service, the waiting No 4549 will be attached to the rear of the train and head the next outbound service. Camping coaches were provided during summer months from 1958 until 1964 and one can be glimpsed beyond the goods shed on the right.

Much of the station was eventually demolished and the site used as a car park. From 23 May 1971 trains terminated on the old goods shed road, where a short (later extended) platform was provided for passenger use. No 150267 is arriving with the 1411 departure from St Erth on 22 September 2008. *Peter W. Gray/DHM*

ST IVES had historically been a busy fishing centre and coastal port but had fallen on hard times before the arrival of the railway, particularly with the collapse of the pilchard fishery. The GWR promoted the town as a tourist resort and in 1878 leased Tregenna Castle, a grand house, for conversion to a hotel. Viewed from Porthminster beach, No 4570 crosses the 10-span viaduct with the 4.12pm service from St Erth on 13 June 1958. The roof of the engine shed can be observed above the third coach; it closed in September 1961 at the end of the summer timetable and North British D63XX diesels were diagrammed to take over most of the branch services from 11 September, though steam continued to see some use for a few more months. *P. K. Tunks*

No 4574 runs round its train on 12 April 1956 after completing the 4¼-mile journey from St Erth. The loop had a capacity of six coaches, though the 2-6-2Ts were normally restricted to hauling 190 tons, the equivalent of five coaches. This could, however, be increased by another vehicle at the expense of an additional minute's running time. *Terry Gough*

127

INDEX OF LOCATIONS

Beacon Siding 6
Bojea Sidings 34
Burngullow 16-21

Camborne 89-91
Carbis Bay 122-125
Carn Brea 86
Carpella 39
Chacewater 80
Cober Viaduct 112
Crugwallins 38

Drinnick Mill area 40-45
Drinnick Mill Junction 40-41
    Low Level 44

Falmouth 77-79

Goonbell Halt and Viaduct 66-67
Goonhavern Halt 62
Grampound Road 22-23
Gwinear Road 6, 92-94

Hayle wharves 115-118
Helston 113-114
High Street Siding 6

Kernick Siding 47

Lansalson 36-37
Lelant 121-122
Lelant Saltings 120
Lower Ruddle Yard 35

Marazion 98-99
Melangoose Mill 50
Meledor Mill 51-53
Mitchell & Newlyn Halt 61
Mithian Halt 65
Mount Hawke Halt 69

Nancegollan 110
Nanpean Wharf 42-43
Newham (Truro) 72
Newquay 56-59
    Harbour 60

Penmere 76
Penryn 75
Penwithers Junction 71
Penzance 104-108
    Ponsandane Yard 103
    shed 100-102

Perranporth 63
    Beach Halt 64
Perranwell 73-74
Praze 109

Quintrel Downs 55

Redruth 81-85
Restowrack Siding 46
Roskear Junction 87
    branch 88

St Agnes 68
St Austell 4, 9-15
St Dennis Junction 48-49, 54
St Erth 95-97, 119
St Ives 126-127

Truro 24-33
    Highertown Tunnel 70
    shed 51-33
Truthall Halt 111-112

Virginia Crossing 50

Despite closing about 45 years previously, certain railway locations are still signposted to help the explorer in 2008! *Both DHM*